Bridge the Gap Lead the Pack

5 Bullet-Proof Ways to Connect and Lead Multi-Generational Teams in the Workplace

Leoni Michael

Dedication

This book was a labor of love, and I would like to dedicate it to my mom and big brother who have gone before us to meet our Savior sooner than any of us would have imagined. They were members of the Leoni fan club and always encouraged me and believed that one day, I would write and publish a book!

To one of the most inspiring men in my life, my daddy who believed in and prayed for all his children, grandchildren, and great grands by name, every Saturday morning, with mom by his side at the breakfast table. Watching them walk in faith even when life would try to beat them down was a gift I will cherish forever.

To my favorite person in entire world, my amazing, God-fearing, supportive, and encouraging husband, Jeff, cheers to us and our commitment to each other and our family! And to my amazing children, McKenzie, Ethan, and Madison… you are the answers to my WHY! #TeamMichael #Partyoffive

Acknowledgments

Thank you, Lord!

I want to express the most heartfelt thank you to my ride or die, amazing sister, Candice for being exactly what I need in a little sis!

Thank you to my circle of friends, you know who you are! I appreciate all the prayers, calls, text messages and words of encouragement when I needed it most.

A big thank you to Wylde Mercy Photography, who happens to be my sister-in-love, Sarah, for my impressive photography, but more importantly, your love and support.

Thank you to our incredibly talented niece, Brenna Sweigard, for her artwork. Your talent is impressive, and I am proud of you!

And a BIG thank you to my writing coach and cohort! You all ROCK!

Table of Contents

Introduction

The Ripple Effect of Connection: How One Leader's Action Changed Lives: From hopeless to high-ranking: The transformation of a woman in her darkest moment

I had just placed a "for lease" sign in front of a home I listed for a client when my phone rang and on the other end was a distressed desperate woman. There were kids in the background and her tearful voice echoed through the phone as she explained her situation - she was a young mother to two adorable little boys, and she was running from an abusive boyfriend. Her plea for help was heartbreaking, and I knew I had to do something (my husband always says, "you don't have to save everyone, but I know you will try, and I know I am coming along").

As a real estate agent, I had built my career on the foundation of building genuine relationships and doing the right thing, even when it didn't result in a financial gain for me. My sweet momma always told us to be the kind of people who treat everyone kindly and with respect even when they can do nothing for you in return. This approach had been instilled in me from an early age, as my family had immigrated to the US with nothing but a suitcase and a dream. We learned to treat everyone with kindness and to help those who couldn't help themselves. Why? Because there are special angels who had done that for me and look where I am today (but that's for another book)!

The woman on the phone was in a dire situation, with no family to turn to and a dangerous ex-boyfriend pursuing her. Her credit was shot, getting approved for anything was nearly impossible without risk, but she had a job and enough money in the bank for one month's rent. I knew I would have zero financial gain (and frankly spending money I didn't have). I also knew I had to help her in any way I could. I shared my own story with her, a story of begging for food at the Amsterdam airport in transit to the U.S and relying on the church and local food banks for our basic needs. At first, she didn't believe me, but with tears welling in my eyes and a look of love and no judgement, I connected with her on a deeply personal level, I offered her hope and faith that things would get better.

That Saturday night, I made sure she had a safe place to stay for a couple of nights and connected her with someone who could help her find a more permanent living situation. I prayed with her, encouraged her, and helped her see her own value and strength.

The transformation that took place in her life (and mine) was nothing short of remarkable. After securing a fresh start, she went on to make significant strides. I saw a strength, determination, and resilience in her that she could see for herself. A few years later, she found me on Facebook to share her successes as she rose to the role of Vice President at a national, get this, staffing company. She later reunited with her family, got married and her boys are now in high school and thriving. Her story had taken a complete turn, thanks to the encouragement and support she received during her darkest moments. In our quest for success, it's easy to get caught up in our own goals, achievements, and profitability.

This experience taught me a valuable lesson that I carry with me every single day. True leadership goes beyond personal gain. It's not about position, title, or our years of experience. It is about using our influence, our position, our experience, and resources to uplift and support those who are struggling to see their value in this world. As you go about your leadership journey, remember that your impact goes far beyond the boardroom.

By connecting with people at their lowest points, showing empathy, and offering unwavering support, we have the power to transform lives. And before you say it (because I know you are thinking it), "this takes so much time Leoni, and we are a business that must be profitable." Keep reading, there is MORE, and it will pay you dividends!

The impact that we create as leaders extends far beyond today. This woman, now a leader in her own right, is paying it forward and bringing hope to others who feel lost and alone. By touching the lives of others in a positive way, we create a ripple effect that can inspire, encourage, and empower generations to come. John Maxwell says, "Connecting increases your influence in every situation. It is the ability to identify with people and relate to them in a way that increases your influence" and once you have that my friend, you have their loyalty and their trust. Winning is a byproduct! And this is the true essence of leadership.

The greatest threat to an organization is the promotion of a high-performing leading with low trust, this is called Toxic Leadership. ~ Leoni Michael

---

This sounds like a whole lot of feelings Leoni. And my answer is, YES it does, but this is a SKILL!

There is a problem in the workplace...It is a problem of values, ambitions, views, mind-sets, demographics, and generations in conflict. In today's workforce, it's important to recognize the value of connecting and building trust with team members from multiple generations. One common mistake I watched leaders make is failing to recognize and celebrate the

4

unique differences and attributes each generation brings to the team. A better understanding of the generations cohabiting the workplace can lead to better recruitment, retention, succession management, communication, employee engagement and conflict resolution. This practice not only fosters a more inclusive and positive work environment, but it also has several tangible benefits for the organization.

Now this is not a deep dive theoretical book focusing on the key tenets of generation theories or on the foundations of generational differences in the workplace (because that is for my dissertation this fall). But I will glean from my education, knowledge acquired through extensive training and certifications, as well as firsthand practical experiences over the years in organizations of all sizes and industries.

Primarily, building trust and connecting with team members of different generations can lead to improved communication. When team members feel comfortable sharing their thoughts and ideas, it can create a more open and collaborative work environment. This concept of sharing thoughts and ideas without fear of retaliation is called psychological safety and this is a term the younger generations understand, so let's start with an inclusive vocabulary and stop digging our heel in on everything new and different to us. Approaching people with opposition because of our expectations and ideology does not mean we have to compromise our values. It simply requires us to connect and communicate effectively.

Additionally, building trust can also lead to enhanced team morale. When team members feel connected and valued, it can boost morale and create a positive work environment. This will result in higher levels of employee satisfaction and retention because they will be happier and engaged in their work, which leads to increased productivity and efficiency. Ultimately, everyone wins!

Another important benefit of connecting with team members from different generations is the opportunity to gain a better understanding of diverse perspectives. Older and younger generations working together in teams can sometimes feel like a tug-of-war. Each generation brings its own unique experiences and insights to the table, and by building trust and connection, team members can learn from one another and make more well-rounded decisions as a result.

Moreover, building trust can facilitate mentorship and learning within the team. Tenured, (older, more mature...quite frankly we should quit being offended by what is true!) team members can share their knowledge and experience with younger colleagues, and vice versa. Instead of drawing our lines in the sand on how to get it done because it is what has worked in the past, why not give a young innovator a crack at it. You never know, they may save you time and money. This life-long learner approach as a leader creates a supportive environment for learning and growth and can ultimately benefit the entire team (I learned how to leverage TikTok and Instagram to promote my biz from these young geniuses!)

Lastly, building trust can help to minimize potential conflicts that may arise from generational differences (tell me you don't see this at least once a day!). I said this earlier, but it truly requires repeating. Conflict is the tension that holds between your expectations, values, pride, and anyone or anything in opposition to that. When we learn and consistently practice the skill of connecting, the harmony on your team will be mind-blowing. You will be known as the "Team Whisperer".

Overall, building trust and connecting with a multi-generational team can improve a leader's effectiveness, because it's the foundation for better understanding and leading diverse team dynamics and individual needs. As a leader, it is important to recognize the value of building these connections and to foster an environment where team members feel valued and supported, regardless of their age or background. There is strength in our differences, and it is a leader's job to find those strengths and to maximize them. By doing so, the organization can benefit from improved communication, increased collaboration, enhanced team morale, and ultimately, the results they desire.

Why should this be important to you?

> *By the beginning of 2024, 53% of employees say they are likely to leave their current employer as confidence in leadership declines. ~Gallup Report*

As a leader, are you maximizing the strengths of the individuals on your team? Do you know what their strengths are? Do you care?

To build a strong workforce for the future and leverage its capabilities, leaders must demonstrate to employees that they are valued for their contribution and commitment. And to do this successfully, leaders must take a human-centered approach to their employees' growth and development and their employer brand.

Let's Bridge the Gap!

Chapter 1.

Crack the Code: Leading a Multi-Generational Dream Team

Understanding and leveraging the unique strengths and skills of employees from different generations is crucial for building a high-performing, cohesive, and successful multi-generational team. In today's workforce, it is not uncommon to have Traditionalists and Baby Boomers working alongside Gen Xers, Millennials, and even Gen Zs. Each generation brings its own set of unique values, work styles, and perspectives to the table, and as a leader, it is your responsibility to ensure that these differences are not only recognized but celebrated and utilized to drive success.

The bullet-proof process is designed to help you bridge the

gap between generations in the workplace and lead the pack to create a dynamic, unstoppable team and create a ripple effect throughout the entire organizational culture. Your new and improved leadership style should permeate every department, team, and person in the organization.

The essence of great leadership is INFLUENCE, not authority. ~Ken Blanchard

The first step starts with understanding YOU! This is essential because as a leader, your level of emotional intelligence will immensely impact your ability to connect and lead employees from different generations. By reflecting on your own EQ, your strengths, and weaknesses, seeking feedback from trusted colleagues, and embracing self-reflective assessments, you can set attainable goals for exponential improvement.

You can become UNSTOPPABLE and bring your people with you.

Understanding how people learn and retain information is crucial for effective leadership, especially when leading multi-generational teams in the workplace. Research shows that people retain information best when they are actively engaged in the learning process. This means that simply reading a book or attending a training session is not enough to ensure that the information is retained and put into practice.

To achieve ultimate retention and implementation of learning or training, there are several key steps that leaders must take. First, it is important to actively engage in the learning process, which may include reading, writing, discussing, and teaching the material to others. This active engagement ensures that the information is processed and retained more effectively.

Studies have shown that reading alone results in a retention rate of only about 10%. However, when individuals both read and write down what they have learned, the retention rate increases to about 20-30%. This shows the importance of actively engaging with the material by writing it down, which promotes better retention and understanding.

If individuals not only read and write, but also discuss the material with others (actively learning with their team members), the retention rate jumps to about 50-70%. This demonstrates the power of verbalizing and exchanging ideas with others to solidify the understanding and retention of the material.

Finally, the ultimate retention and implementation of learning occurs when individuals not only read, write, and discuss, but also teach back the material they have learned to others. This method has been proven to result in a retention rate jumping to about 90-95%, highlighting the importance of reinforcing and solidifying one's understanding through teaching others.

This is where you can shine as a leader. Create an environment of learning and growing, create a culture of sharing knowledge, create a team that will follow their leader's example of empowerment. Leaders should not only read this book but put its principles into practice to lead effective and productive, dynamic multi-generational teams in the workplace.

Lead your Pack!

Practicing self-awareness techniques will enhance your emotional intelligence. By understanding your own emotions and how they impact your leadership style, you will be better equipped to connect with and lead employees of all ages (and this transformational strategy can work at home too).

Understanding each generation's values and work styles is the next critical step. By conducting research, engaging in open discussions, and seeking out resources on generational differences, you will gain valuable insights into what motivates and drives each generation. By keeping an open mind and avoiding making assumptions about employees based on their generational background, you can build a solid foundation for effective leadership. It may feel like you're communicating with aliens sometimes but truthfully, understanding the basics about each generation will improve everything!

Building trust, fostering open communication, providing

12

coaching and mentoring, promoting collaboration and teamwork, and leading by example are all crucial elements that contribute to creating a workplace culture where employees from different generations can thrive. By following this step-by-step process, you will not only gain a deeper understanding of the unique strengths and skills of employees from different generations but also create an environment where diversity is celebrated, and everyone feels valued and respected.

By leveraging the unique strengths of all employees, you will unlock the full potential of your team and gain a competitive edge in the marketplace. So, if you are ready to bridge the generation gap in the workplace and lead a multi-generational team to success, this book is your go-to guide. The strategies outlined here will equip you with the tools and knowledge you need to connect and lead employees of all ages in all directions (leading up, down, or across generations), ultimately creating a workplace where everyone can thrive and maximize their full potential.

As a leader, you need to remember that when you accept the responsibility of leadership, you no longer sell the products or services, you are now responsible to build the team of people who will sell the products or services.

Buckle Up and Trust the Process!

Chapter 2.

Know Yourself, Lead Others: Leveraging Emotional Intelligence in the Workplace

This chapter will help you:

1. Understand the importance of emotional intelligence in leadership and why leaders in the workplace struggle with it.

2. Understand Daniel Goleman's 5 components of emotional intelligence and their significance in effective leadership.

3. Reflect on your own emotional intelligence strengths and weaknesses to facilitate personal growth as a leader.

4. Understand the benefits of modeling a learning attitude

and the desire for self-improvement as a leader.

5. Understand the importance of seeking valuable feedback from trusted colleagues, family, and friends to gain insight into how others perceive you at home and work and identify your blind spots.

In today's fast-paced and ever-changing workplace, emotional intelligence is becoming increasingly crucial for leaders who want to build cohesive, high-performing multi-generational teams. Emotional intelligence is a key factor in connecting and leading multi-generations, and by the end of this chapter, you will have a clear understanding of how to define and leverage your own emotional intelligence to lead effectively.

Stop for about 2 minutes and answer these two questions:
What are you doing to develop yourself?
What are you doing to develop others?

_____

_____

_____

_____

_____

_____

_____

Understand Emotional Intelligence and Why it Start with You

Leaders in the workplace are frustrated with themselves and their employees, yet they fear vulnerability, emotional discussions, and training on one of the most important soft skills in life: Emotional Intelligence (also referred to as EQ). As leaders, we'd like to believe that people quit jobs and companies because of money, other factors and that it has nothing to do with us. Yet, statistics tell us a different, true story and that is that 65% of people who leave their jobs will tell you it is because of their manager. **People don't quit jobs or organizations, people quit PEOPLE!** All reasons lead back to leadership.

Emotional intelligence is the ability to understand and manage your own emotions, as well as the emotions of others. It involves empathy, self-awareness, self-regulation, motivation, and social skills. Many leaders are frustrated with themselves and their employees because they lack the ability to connect on an emotional level, leading to miscommunication and conflict in the workplace.

We need to reject the narrative that being vulnerable and too emotional at work is a sign of weakness, but instead embrace that we are all people and operate on emotion. People desire connection and a higher level of emotional intelligence in their leaders because it fosters trust, empathy, and effective communication which can lead to better decision-making, stronger relationships, and improved team performance.

This Boss Broke All the "Normal Corporate" Rules to Save Her Employee - And It Worked

I remember the day Madison, the once bright and enthusiastic, full of life employee, was placed on a performance improvement plan. At that time, I was working as the director of the department, a position I had been promoted to after starting out as an individual contributor and a former coworker who I will call Madison. It was a difficult situation to navigate, especially since I had built a connection with her long before becoming her boss. I saw her struggling to keep up with her duties, to be present, and to find joy in her work every day like she did when she first started working with us. It was clear that something was going on in her life, but it was not my place to address it until I became her leader.

There were weeks of back and forth with HR, Madison's

immediate supervisor and the former director. They provided me with details of her performance issues. I wasn't naïve to dismiss all her mistakes, but I also realized she wasn't getting a fair assessment due to lack of leadership. I struggled with the decision to put her on a performance improvement plan and why did I have to be the one to take this step, when her inability to perform had occurred on my former director's watch? At the time I could not shake the feeling that it wasn't fair for me to be the one making this decision, but you will soon find out why I am thankful it was me after all.

You see, I knew the potential Madison had, and I understood the difficulties she was going through because I asked and listened empathetically. I had always taken the time to build a relationship with my colleagues. I genuinely cared about them, wanted to understand their lives outside of work, and listen to their struggles. And Madison was no exception. Even before I became her boss, I was invested in her well-being.

So, instead of immediately following through with the PIP, I took a different approach and sat down with her to engage in a direct and honest conversation. I needed to understand why she was struggling at work. I invested even more time in helping her and her direct supervisor, mediating conflicts, listening with empathy, and coaching them both in building a more productive work relationship. I knew that she was capable of more, and she just needed someone to show up for her and empower her.

Madison needed time to speak, to be heard, to be understood. It was not my natural inclination to be so patient at work because I am such an intense, high-strung personality always wanting to win, but I realized that she needed a calm, patient boss at that time. I led with empathy, an open mind, and a listening ear. And she responded well to that approach. Madison trusted me and her desire to improve led to the turning point. She and I went into the meeting with HR, and despite their low expectations for a comeback, we both knew that there was still hope for her. We produced a winning game plan, and I believed her when she told me she wanted to win. I was committed to helping her find that winning spirit within herself again.

So, we worked together, harder than ever. I coached her, encouraged her, and spent countless hours with her. And slowly, but surely, things began to change. She rose above the challenges, the doubts, the naysayers, and the setbacks.

When I left the company, Madison left too. It wasn't because of me, but because she felt that it was time for a fresh start. She said the only person who believed in her and treated her with love and care was no longer there so why stay at a place where the remaining leaders did not believe in her. She found a job at a new company that immediately recognized her value, and they gave her the fresh start she deserved. She is thriving and I am incredibly proud of her.

The lesson from this experience is that sometimes, being a

leader means taking the *TIME* to truly understand others, to listen, and to believe in them, which can make all the difference. I could have easily followed through with the standard procedure and placed Madison on the performance improvement plan, let the 90 days run its course and then move on, but I knew that would not have achieved the same result.

---

*The enemy of success is **your comfort zone** (your resistance to change), **learned helplessness** (I cannot change), and **the path of least resistance** (the easy way out).*

The Foundation of Emotional Intelligence

Today, many forward-thinking companies are actively promoting and cultivating emotional intelligence as an integral part of their workplace culture. Companies understand that a workforce with strong emotional intelligence can navigate challenges more effectively and contribute to a healthier work environment.

My Enthusiastic Plea: "Stop Putting Lipstick on a Pig"

I've been a real estate agent for the last 17 years and if there is one thing I learned very early on in my career as an agent regarding the homes in Texas; you either currently have a foundation problem, you had a foundation problem, or you will have a foundation problem. And most people will only want to plaster the cracks and then paint over them, redo the flooring, and paint over it all. You know the whole lipstick on a pig deal! Why? Because it is cheaper and faster. But that does not fix the root of the problem and the symptoms will reappear.

I cannot help but draw parallels to the world of leadership and organizations. Just like a house, an organization needs a strong, emotionally intelligent foundation to withstand the adverse conditions that cause organizational cracks, disruptions, shifts and in worse cases, the crumbling of a once strong culture. In today's corporate culture, leaders are facing major challenges such as losing notable talent, they struggle to motivate, connect, and lead multi-generations in the workplace.

I believe the key to building a solid foundation in organizations lies in a shift in mindset for leaders who are willing to try something new. Leaders who possess high emotional intelligence, humility, and a radical respect for their employees will be the ones to take the next generations to greater heights. The stronger your leadership foundation, the higher you can all go!

It is about building teams on a solid foundation of trust, respect, and understanding. By understanding and valuing emotional intelligence, leaders can not only connect with and lead multiple generations in the workplace, but also create a culture where everyone feels heard, respected, and valued.

Let's commit to reinforcing the foundation that will withstand future harsh elements threatening the integrity of your organization.

What is Emotional Intelligence?

Daniel Goleman introduced the concept of Emotional Intelligence (EQ), and it played a pivotal role in introducing EQ to the broader audience and forward-thinking organizations ran with the positive impact of the adoption of the five components of emotional intelligence (EQ). This was the new foundation as an effective tool for hiring, promoting, employee development, leading and overall organizational success.

One example of a company that has successfully adapted to EQ in the workplace is **Salesforce.** They have been recognized for their commitment to social responsibility and their efforts to create a diverse and inclusive workplace. Millennials and Gen Z's (and even my generation, Gen X-ers) are flocking to work for organizations like these because of a workplace culture that has been praised for its flexible work arrangements, which include remote work and flexible scheduling. Salesforce offers opportunities for continuous growth and development, and it has a strong focus on corporate citizenship.

Let me give you the cliff notes of each component as it plays a unique role in improving leadership skills, building strong relationships, and fostering a positive workplace culture. When leaders possess an elevated level of emotional intelligence, they are better equipped to understand and manage their own emotions, as well as the emotions of others, leading to more successful leadership outcomes.

#1 Self-Awareness:

Leaders who are self-aware are in tune with their emotions, strengths, and weaknesses. By developing self-awareness, you can better understand how your emotions and actions impact those around you. Self-aware leaders can recognize and manage their emotions in high-pressure situations, leading to more effective decision-making and communication with their team.

The Cautionary Tale of a Leader's Lack of Self-Awareness

I worked at an organization with a colleague who led an exceptionally large team of entry-level salespeople. His team consisted of approximately forty individuals from all walks of life and different generations. This leader, who I will refer to as Tom, thought he was incredibly self-aware and honestly believed that he had a great connection with the people he led. He believed that his dictatorship style (which he would be offended by calling it that) of leading and his brutally honest approach would help his team make better sales and increase their numbers. But what he didn't realize was the negative impact he was having on everyone around him, and his style of communication and leadership was detrimental to the people and the organization.

One thing that drove me insane about Tom was when he needed something from you, you were on his timetable. Even then, when you tried to connect with him, give him the information he needed, or explain yourself, he would cut you off mid-sentence and talk over you. When he was done, the conversation was pretty much over, regardless of where you were in your explanation. I was not the only one affected by this.

I vividly remember his employees coming to me, expressing their frustration with the way he treated them. When they approached him, he denied it and would retaliate by micromanaging them even more. This cycle of disregard and disrespect continued, and the organization did nothing about it, simply because he had been employed with them for over 20 years.

There was no resolution, and the negative impact he had on the employees was palpable. Many felt afraid to speak up for themselves in fear of retaliation, they felt demotivated, leaving them frustrated and defeated. This not only affected their work life but also their personal lives, as they took stress and anxiety home with them.

The moral of the story is that Tom was not a bad person outside of work. However, his behaviors at work reflected his interactions in his personal life as well. His lack of self-awareness came across as arrogance, and it had a lasting and destructive impact on those around him. The negative environment he created at work bled into the personal lives of his employees, affecting their families and overall well-being. Now I know some generations have the mindset that we need to toughen up in the workplace, but this kind of response can be a mistake because it assumes everyone has the same emotional and mental capacity for "toughness."

In the end, the takeaway from this experience is the importance of self-awareness and understanding the impact our actions have on others. Tom's self-absorbed behavior not only affected his team's work performance, but it also took a toll on their personal lives. It serves as a reminder that our actions and behaviors have a ripple effect on the people around us. The story of Tom serves as a cautionary tale to always be mindful of how we treat others and the influence we have on those around us.

Why Self-Awareness Matters: 7 Compelling Reasons to Look Within

- It allows us to recognize our strengths and weaknesses, enabling us to take steps to develop and improve ourselves.

- Self-awareness helps us to recognize patterns in our behavior and identify potential areas for growth and change.

- It allows us to understand our values and beliefs, helping us to make decisions that align with our true selves.

- Self-awareness can lead to increased confidence and self-esteem, as we have a better understanding of our abilities and potential.

- It helps us to make more authentic and meaningful connections with others, as we can show up as our true selves.

- Self-awareness can lead to increased resilience and adaptability, as we are better able to cope with change and challenges.

- It enables us to live a more purposeful and meaningful life, as we can align our actions with our values and goals.

On a scale of 1-5, how self-aware are you? How did you measure your answer? Have you ever asked co-workers, your team, your boss, or family members to rate you?

_____

_____

_____

_____

_____

_____

_____

7 Practical Strategies for Success in Self-Awareness

- Recognize the impact of your emotions on your decision-making and interactions with others.

- Take time for self-reflection and introspection to better understand your own thoughts and feelings.

- Seek feedback from trusted colleagues and mentors to gain insights into how others perceive you.

- Use tools such as personality assessments or 360-degree feedback to gain a deeper understanding of your strengths and areas for growth.

- Be open to acknowledging and addressing blind spots or areas of personal development.

- Pay attention to physical cues and reactions that may be indicative of underlying emotions.

- Avoid self-sabotage: With self-awareness, individuals can recognize self-destructive behaviors and habits, and take proactive steps to overcome them.

Was there a time when you hurt someone you were leading due to your lack of self-awareness? How did it make you feel?

_____

_____

_____

_____

_____

_____

_____

#2 Self-Control:

This involves the ability to control impulsive feelings and behaviors and adapt to changing circumstances with ease. This is the EQ muscle that allows you to remain calm and composed in challenging situations. *For example,* an employee makes a mistake and the first thing that comes to your mind and out of your mouth is, "what in the world were you thinking" or "sometimes I think I am better off doing things myself around here", followed by a quick apology. Well, the damage is done. You cannot un-ring a bell and words are powerful.

Leaders who exhibit strong self-regulation are less likely to react rashly in difficult situations, leading to a more stable and consistent leadership approach. This emotional self-control can positively impact the work environment and inspire trust and confidence in the leader.

Why Self-Control is the Secret to Your Career Advancement: 7 Key Reasons

- *Better decision-making* - self-control helps employees make more rational and thoughtful decisions, leading to better outcomes for the company.

- *Increased productivity* – Self-regulation allows employees to stay focused and manage their time effectively to stay on task and avoid distractions.

- *Improved teamwork* - self-regulated individuals are more likely to consider the needs and perspectives of their coworkers, leading to better collaboration and communication.

- *Reduced conflict* - employees with self-control are better able to manage their emotions and oversee conflicting situations in a professional manner.

- *Enhanced leadership abilities* - self-regulated individuals are better able to set and achieve goals, showing initiative and motivating others to do the same.

- *Better work-life balance* - self-regulated individuals are better able to manage their workload and avoid burnout, leading to a healthier work-life balance for themselves and their colleagues.

- *Increased job satisfaction* - employees with self-regulation feel more in control of their work and are more satisfied with their jobs as a result.

Was there ever a time in your career or personal life where you lost your cool and deeply hurt someone and broke their spirit or your relationship with them? How did it make you feel?

_____

_____

_____

_____

_____

_____

_____

Master Self-Control: 7 Strategies for Success

- Set specific, achievable goals for yourself, track your progress regularly, and develop a routine, and stick to it to build discipline and consistency in your actions.

- Avoid temptations and triggers that may lead to impulsive behavior.

- Get enough sleep and prioritize self-care that includes regular physical activity to improve impulse control, cognitive functioning, and reduce stress.

- Use positive self-talk and affirmations to empower yourself and stay focused on your goals.

- Learn to delay gratification and resist immediate rewards in favor of long-term benefits.

- Practice saying no to things that don't align with your goals and values.

- Engage in regular physical activity to improve impulse control and cognitive functioning.

What can you start doing today to avoid losing control of your team or colleagues?

_____

_____

_____

_____

_____

_____

_____

EQ is not about managing your emotions; it is about managing your reaction to your emotion.

#3 Motivation:

Motivation is essential for effective leadership. Leaders who are intrinsically motivated, enthusiastic, and committed to their goals can inspire their team members to work towards a common vision. By fostering a culture of motivation and enthusiasm, you can improve team productivity and drive them to achieve greater success beyond the workplace. Later, I will touch on motivations for each generation in the workplace.

 Watch this video on Motivation:
https://www.youtube.com/watch?v=i1fXAmAp
PrA&ab_channel=Motivation2Study

Unleashing the Power of Motivation: Understanding How it Works

- Motivation is the driving force that moves people to take action.

- It can be *intrinsic,* stemming from internal factors such as personal values, interests, and emotions, or *extrinsic*, influenced by external rewards and consequences... money talks!

- Motivation can be influenced by biological, psychological, and social factors, such as genetics, personality traits, and social norms.

- The role of dopamine, a neurotransmitter associated with pleasure and reward, has been linked to motivation and goal-directed behavior.

- Self-determination theory proposes that people are motivated when their needs for autonomy, achievement, affiliation, power, competence, and relatedness are fulfilled.

- Goal-setting theory suggests that specific, challenging, and achievable goals can increase motivation and performance.

- Expectancy theory posits that people are motivated when they believe their efforts will lead to desired outcomes and rewards.

- Achievement motivation theory explores how individuals are driven to strive for success and avoid failure in various life domains.

- Maslow's hierarchy of needs highlights the different levels of motivation that individuals experience as they seek to satisfy their physiological, safety, social, esteem, and self-actualization needs.

- Motivation can fluctuate based on factors such as fatigue, stress, and mood, as well as changing external circumstances and environmental cues.

- Positive reinforcement, such as praise and rewards, can enhance motivation, while negative reinforcement, such as criticism and punishment, may decrease motivation.

- Understanding the principles of motivation can help individuals and organizations create effective strategies to inspire and engage people in achieving their goals.

What motivates you? What motivates each team member that you currently lead? Do you know? How can you find out?

McKenzie, what motivates your Millennial generation in the workplace?

Strategies on Cracking the Code of Human Motivation

- Understand the different individual motivators of team members, such as recognition, autonomy, and growth opportunities.

- Take the time to actively listen to team members' feedback and concerns. ***Actively listening*** is making eye contact with the person, nodding to indicate you are tracking, repeating back what you hear them saying.

- Develop empathy and the ability to understand and relate to others' emotions and experiences.

- Communicate openly and transparently with team members to build trust and understanding.

- Recognize and celebrate team members' achievements and milestones.

- Offer opportunities for professional development and growth within the organization.

- Foster a positive and inclusive workplace culture that values diversity and inclusion.

- Take the time to understand each team member's strengths and areas for growth.

- Provide clear and achievable goals for team members to strive towards.

- Encourage a collaborative and supportive work environment that promotes teamwork.

- Recognize and address any sources of dissatisfaction or disengagement among team members.

- Demonstrate flexibility and adaptability in response to individual team members' preferences.

- Foster an environment where constructive feedback is welcomed and utilized for personal and professional growth.

- Lead by example and demonstrate the qualities of emotional intelligence in your own interactions and decisions.

- Continuously seek feedback and self-reflect on your own emotional intelligence and leadership practices.

How do you feel about taking the time to invest in people in this manner? How do you view taking the time out of your day or week to invest in your people?

_____

_____

_____

_____

_____

_____

#4 Empathy:

Leaders who are empathetic can understand and relate to the emotions and experiences of others. This allows you to build stronger connections between you and your team members and create a more supportive and inclusive environment that fosters a sense of belonging and trust within the team, allowing for open communication, respect, and a supportive work culture. Here are several compelling reasons why leaders should prioritize and cultivate empathy in the workplace.

Empathetic Leadership: 10 Examples of How It Impacts Employee Engagement, Performance and Retention

- Increases employee satisfaction and loyalty.

- Improves team communication and collaboration.

- Enhances leadership effectiveness and credibility as it builds trust and rapport with employees.

- Fosters a positive and inclusive work environment.

- Builds trust and rapport with employees.

- Reduces conflicts and misunderstandings.

- Improves employee retention and reduces turnover.

- Strengthens relationships and rapport with clients and

customers.

- Improves decision-making by considering the perspective of others.

- Enhances the ability to motivate and inspire employees.

- Helps leaders to be more attuned to the emotional and mental well-being of their team.

The Empathetic Leader's Toolbox: 10 Proven Methods for Creating a High-Performance Culture

- Practice active listening - truly pay attention to what employees are saying and validate their feelings and experiences.

- Show empathy by putting yourself in your employees' shoes and understanding their perspective.

- Encourage open communication and create a supportive and inclusive work environment where employees feel comfortable expressing their emotions, concerns, thoughts, and ideas. *Just because you don't "do" feelings at work, doesn't mean your employees have the same perspective.*

- Lead by example and demonstrate empathy in your interactions with others.

- Offer flexibility and when possible, accommodate to support employees' individual needs and challenges.

- Acknowledge great work and express gratitude for their hard work and contributions.

- Provide opportunities for professional development and growth and show understanding and excitement of employees' career aspirations and goals.

- Offer resources and support for mental health and well-being, recognizing the impact it has on employee engagement and performance.

- Be transparent and honest in your communication and show vulnerability as a leader to build trust and connection. *This idea of vulnerability makes many uncomfortable, but it really is the magic bullet!*

- Recognize and celebrate the diverse perspectives and experiences of your team members and promote inclusivity and diversity.

*** Recall the story I mentioned earlier about the young lady who I had to place on a PIP? That is a prime example of the power of an empathetic leader. I allowed her the space to be vulnerable and I was vulnerable with her as I shared my experiences and struggles with her. I am not saying you need to get so intimate with your employees where you cross professional lines, but vulnerability is showing your people

you are human too and you get them! ***

#5 Social Skills:

 Leaders with strong social skills are adept at building relationships, managing conflicts, and inspiring others. By effectively communicating and collaborating with their team, leaders can create a positive and cohesive work environment. Social skills are crucial for successful leadership, as they foster teamwork, open communication, and a powerful sense of unity among team members. So, let's not draw this out and get to the bottom line:

The Top 7 Benefits of Having Strong Social Skills in a Leadership Role

- *Resilience*: Strong social skills enable leaders to bounce back from setbacks and maintain a positive attitude, inspiring their team to do the same.

- *Trust and respect*: Leaders with strong social skills earn the trust and respect of their team members, fostering loyalty and commitment.

- *Adaptability*: Socially adept leaders can navigate and manage change more effectively, leading their teams through transitions and challenges.

- *Culture and morale:* Leadership social skills are essential for creating and maintaining a positive, inclusive, and empowering workplace culture, boosting employee morale and satisfaction.

- *Effective communication*: Leadership social skills are vital in the workplace as they enable leaders to communicate effectively with their team members, ensuring that messages are clearly understood, and objectives are met.

- *Conflict resolution*: Strong leadership social skills help in resolving conflicts among team members, creating a harmonious and productive work environment.

- *Team building:* Leaders with strong social skills can build cohesive and high-performing teams through effective collaboration and communication.

The Weaknesses of EQ

While emotional intelligence is an essential aspect of effective leadership, it is not without its weaknesses. For instance, an overemphasis on emotions and empathy can sometimes lead to decision-making that is overly influenced by personal biases and feelings. Additionally, individuals with high EQ may struggle with setting boundaries and making tough decisions that prioritize the overall success of the team. Finally, leaders who lack emotional intelligence may have difficulty connecting with their team members, leading to disengagement and a lack of trust in their leadership.

Understanding the weaknesses can lead to more effective leadership for multiple generations in the workplace. By recognizing the limitations of emotional intelligence, leaders can supplement their EQ with other essential skills and strategies. *For example,* combining emotional intelligence with strategic thinking, decisiveness, and resilience can lead to more balanced and effective leadership. Additionally, being aware of the potential pitfalls of EQ can help leaders navigate diverse teams with different communication styles and emotional needs.

Developing and refining the five components of emotional intelligence can greatly improve your leadership abilities. By cultivating self-awareness, self-regulation, motivation, empathy, and social skills, you can create a more cohesive and productive work environment. And while emotional intelligence has its limitations, knowing and understanding these weaknesses can lead to more effective leadership for multi-generations in the workplace, as leaders are better equipped to understand and connect with individuals of all backgrounds and experiences. By embracing a balanced approach to leadership that integrates emotional intelligence with other essential skills, you can inspire, empower, and guide your team towards success.

Leaders complain that the team is not carrying their load. But if you ask the team, nine times out of ten it is because they don't have a good shepherd. They lack intentional expectations of growth, and it is the leader's responsibility to set the expectation.

Bonus Exercise

Reflecting on Your Emotional Intelligence Strengths and Weaknesses

I use these questions in my coaching practice and find it incredibly helpful when my clients do not know where to begin on this journey of self-discovery.

Take time to reflect on your own emotional intelligence. What are your strengths and weaknesses in each of the five components? Being honest with yourself about your emotional intelligence is essential for growth and improvement as a leader.

Self-Awareness

- How in tune am I with my own emotions?

- Do I take the time to recognize and understand what I am feeling and how those emotions are impacting my thoughts and behaviors?

- Am I able to accurately identify my strengths and weaknesses, as well as my values and beliefs? What are they?

_____

_____

_____

_____

_____

_____

_____

Self-Regulation

- How well do I manage my emotions and impulses?

- Am I able to remain calm and composed in challenging situations, or do my emotions tend to get the best of me? How?

- Do I practice mindfulness and self-control in my everyday life? How?

- How do I manage stress and anxiety?

_____

_____

_____

_____

_____

_____

_____

Motivation

- What inspires and drives me to achieve my goals?

- Am I able to maintain a positive attitude and persistence, even in the face of setbacks and obstacles? If not, what is my go-to emotion or reaction?

- Do I find joy and fulfillment in my work and personal pursuits? Describe?

- How can I cultivate a greater sense of purpose and passion in my life? Do I even know what my passions and purpose are?

- What is driving me right now? Why?

_____

_____

_____

_____

_____

_____

_____

Empathy

- How well do I understand and connect with the emotions of others?

- Do I care what others are saying or do I cut people off to hear myself speak because I know a lot?

- Am I able to show compassion and consideration towards the feelings and perspectives of those around me?

- Do I actively listen and seek to understand, rather than jumping to conclusions or judgment? How?

_____

_____

_____

_____

_____

_____

_____

Social Skills

- How effectively do I communicate and interact with others?

- Am I able to build and maintain strong relationships? How?

- Do I build relationships with people because of what they can do for me or what I can do for them?

- Am I skilled in conflict resolution and negotiation? How do I know I am successful in this skill?

- Do I work well in teams and adapt to various social situations with ease? If not, why?

_____

_____

_____

_____

_____

_____

Benefits of Leading the Charge and Setting the Tone

By modeling a learning attitude and the desire for your own self-improvement first, you can inspire and lead your team to excellence. Embracing a growth mindset and your commitment to learning and improving yourself first, sets a powerful example for your team. One of the greatest teachers of leadership and growth is my friend and mentor, John Maxwell. One of the very first books I read by John is, *The 21 Irrefutable Laws of Leadership* and the second book, and by far my favorite, *The 15 Invaluable Laws of Growth.*

John says *potential* is a word that "invokes hope, it hints greatness, it looks forward with optimism" and to not live your fullest potential is "like dying with the music still inside of you". You see, what I learned from John was that to grow in my potential, I first need to grow in my self-awareness because my potential is within.

You cannot *lead the pack* if you cannot lead yourself first.

You cannot grow others to their fullest potential if YOU don't have a growth mindset for yourself.

Leadership is not a title or position you earned; it is a responsibility. Be intentional with growing yourself and your

---

Change is inevitable. Growth is optional ~ John Maxwell

---

team. Model a learning attitude.

Seeking Feedback from Trusted Colleagues, Family, and Friends

Feedback is a valuable tool for growth. Seeking feedback from trusted colleagues, family, and friends is crucial for personal and professional growth. The insights and perspectives of others can provide valuable guidance and help us see things from a different angle. Whether it's a project at work, a personal goal, or a creative endeavor, feedback can offer constructive criticism and encouragement that can only make us better.

Feedback helps us to gain a fresh perspective on our work. Sometimes, we can get so focused on our own ideas and opinions that we lose sight of the bigger picture. Seeking feedback allows us to step back and see things from a different angle, which can lead to new insights and ideas that we may not have thought of on our own.

Additionally, feedback can help us identify blind spots and areas for improvement. We all have things that we cannot see about ourselves, whether it's a weakness in our work or a character flaw. Trusted colleagues, family, and friends can provide honest and constructive feedback that can help us grow and develop in areas we may not have even realized needed improvement. For example, you might ask a colleague how they perceive your ability to manage conflict in the workplace.

Finally, feedback can also provide validation and encouragement. When we share our work with others and receive positive feedback, it can validate our efforts and boost our confidence. On the flip side, constructive criticism can help us refine our work and strive for better results. In both cases, seeking feedback can be a source of inspiration and motivation to keep pushing forward – it can only make you better.

Take an EQ Assessment - Set Goals for Improvement

Have you ever heard of a 360-assessment? This powerful tool allows individuals to gain insight into their strengths and areas for development by collecting feedback from multiple perspectives, such as supervisors, peers, and direct reports. It is a comprehensive way to gather information about your performance, leadership style, and interpersonal skills. The

360-assessment can unveil blind spots and help you understand how others perceive you, giving you the knowledge you need to grow and excel in your career.

In addition to the 360-assessment, the EQ-i 2.0 assessment is an incredible resource for individuals looking to improve their emotional intelligence (EQ). This assessment measures emotional and social functioning, providing insights into areas such as self-awareness, empathy, and stress management. It can help you understand your emotional strengths and areas for development, ultimately leading to improved relationships, better decision-making, and enhanced leadership abilities.

If you are interested in taking these assessments, there are many resources available online and through certified professionals. You can find 360-assessments through HR departments, leadership development programs, or by collaborating with a coach or consultant. As for the EQ-i 2.0 assessment, it is often administered and debriefed by certified professionals who are trained to interpret the results and provide personalized recommendations for growth.

Remember, these assessments are not about judgment or criticism—they are about empowerment and self-improvement. So, embrace the opportunity to learn more about yourself and take the necessary steps to further develop your skills. After all, personal growth is a lifelong journey, and these assessments can be powerful tools to help you along the way.

Set Your Goals

Let's be SMART and set specific, measurable, achievable, relevant, and timely goals for improving your emotional intelligence based on the feedback and assessment results. Whether it's practicing active listening, managing stress more effectively, or practicing empathy in challenging situations, having clear goals will guide your growth.

As you work through these points, consider grabbing a cup of coffee and finding a quiet place to reflect on your feelings. Try journaling your thoughts and feelings and be open to feedback from your *trusted* colleagues, friends, and family members.

Remember, developing emotional intelligence takes time and effort. Understanding and leveraging EQ is a key factor in leading multi-generational teams effectively. By taking the time to reflect on your own emotional intelligence, seeking feedback, and setting goals for improvement, you can create a solid foundation and you, and the people you lead will win at work and at home. Keep an open mind, be kind to yourself, and embrace the journey of self-improvement.

Good luck, you got this!

Chapter 3:

Understanding Values, Motivations, and Work Styles for Effective Leadership

This chapter will help you:

1. Understand the values, motivations, and work styles of different generations in your team allowing you to tailor your leadership approach and embrace a genuine desire to learn and grow alongside your multi-generational team.

2. Utilize the DiSC assessment to understand how others communicate.

3. Utilize the components of EQ (self-regulation, motivation, empathy, social skills) to connect with team

members of different generations such as Baby Boomers valuing loyalty and hard work while Generation X values independence and work-life balance.

4. Learn how to create a workplace culture that respects and leverages the unique strengths of each generation, leading to higher employee satisfaction, improved teamwork, and a thriving, unstoppable multi-generational team.

The Power of Assessments: How Understanding Personalities Transformed a Work Environment

I was working at a global company, serving as the director of Learning and Development while also functioning as a Coach. This was a new concept for the organization, as they did not have anyone with my skill set in Education and Training. However, the leaders and managers at the company were hungry for something different. They understood their current practices were no longer working.

One day, a senior director of a department approached me, seeking my help to save his team and potentially his own reputation. The backstory was that he, along with his managers, had previously participated (on separate occasions) in a four-day management workshop where I taught leaders about emotional intelligence, understanding human behavior, motivations, work styles, values, and how to build trusting work relationships.

The director knew the potential of the tools and techniques I taught, and he truly trusted my skills; he had noticed minor individual changes in himself and his managers after they attended my workshops. However, the managers were having a tough time seeing eye-to-eye on everything and I do mean anything.

The work environment was becoming so toxic due to the lack of synergy and effective communication among them. This situation escalated to the point where employees were filing formal complaints with HR, and the director knew he needed to make a notable change. He approached me as a final-ditch effort to help him resolve the issue.

With immense passion for coaching people, I wholeheartedly accepted the challenge. I set up a mediation coaching session with the managers, the director, and myself. We spent an hour hashing it out. I began by emphasizing the importance of listening; empathetic, genuine listening, which no one was doing at this time.

As we delved deeper, we addressed the personal motivations, values, and work styles of each person. Walls of distrust were broken down as we uncovered the reasons behind their conflicts and anxieties. We discovered a shared goal - the success of the organization and the genuine love they each had for their roles and their teams.

The transformation in the room was remarkable. Everyone began empathetically listening to one another. We learned about one another's motivations, values, and the discomforts that had led to the conflict. I could see the understanding and awareness growing within the group.

Reflecting on this experience, I thought back to the workshops I had conducted, particularly the day spent on the DiSC assessment. This 30-page report provided valuable insights into each person's natural inclinations, communication styles, strengths, and weaknesses. Utilizing this assessment had allowed me to coach each leader in a way that was tailored to their unique personality traits and communication preferences while pointing out potential downfalls and weaknesses in a non-threatening manner.

For example, one of the managers had a dominant, I will do it myself, data-driven personality, but was honestly, a kind-hearted person once you cracked the code to her heartstrings. I coached the other manager to understand her personality style and how they could work together effectively. Similarly, I navigated the clash of dominant traits between the other two managers, enabling them to work together in harmony.

The key takeaway from this experience is the power of using assessments not as a weapon against one's team, but as a tool to foster better communication, understanding, and teamwork. Through a shared understanding of each other's strengths and weaknesses, we were able to build a foundation of trust and cooperation that ultimately transformed the team dynamic for the better.

This is the email I received from the director just a week later!

"Leoni, I just wanted to thank you for coaching my leadership team last week. If you did not step in, I am not sure where we would be today. But because you did and you were amazing in facilitating productive conversations, I already see a change in them. The team even noticed a change and asked me if everything was okay. LOL. Your skill in listening and coaching is exceptional, and you taught me how to navigate difficult conversations. You are impressive ma'am and I just wanted you to know that we are so lucky to have someone like you. ~ Mike"

You will win in this chapter if you can have:

An open mind: It is necessary for leaders to approach the process of understanding and connecting with different generations in the team without biases or preconceived notions.

No judgment of any generation: It is important for leaders to approach the differences in values and work styles of different generations without passing judgment, to foster a more inclusive and empathetic work environment.

A sense of humor: It can help leaders navigate through the differences in values and work styles with a positive and light-hearted approach, promoting a more harmonious and collaborative work environment.

The Mass Exodus of Earlier Retirements: Why Traditional Leadership Strategies are Failing in a Multi-Generational Workplace

Every day, I found myself in the middle of what felt like a battlefield in the workplace, fighting to bridge the gap between employees of all generations. Right after the pandemic in 2020, the workplace dynamics seemed to have shifted drastically. The frustration was palpable, and people came to me seeking coaching, advice, and reassurance as they struggled to navigate the new normal.

I remember having conversations with Baby Boomer and Silent Generation employees, who expressed their frustration and saying, "I think it's time to retire early. I don't understand the work ethic and motivations of these younger kids. It's hard to have a conversation with them, to really understand them."

On the other hand, Millennials and Gen Zs approached me with the same sentiment - feeling misunderstood and unappreciated by the older generations, saying, "I don't think Bob likes me. I think I irritate him, and I just want to get to know him and learn from him."

It became apparent that there was a growing gap between the different generations in the workplace, a gap that needed to be bridged. As we eased into a new normal and adapted to the changing dynamics of the workplace, the question became, "Where do we go from here?" It was essential to find a way to bring all the generations together, to ensure productivity, profitability, and successful relationship building for the generations to come.

The conflict between the generations resulted in people retiring earlier than expected, leaving with a wealth of knowledge and experience. Meanwhile, the younger generation was left feeling clueless about how to navigate corporate life and learn the essential skills needed for success. It was evident that there was a pressing need to address the communication breakdown and bridge the gap between the generations.

This realization ignited a passion within me. Despite the differences, we were all saying the same thing, experiencing the same challenges in different worlds. By embracing empathy, understanding, and open communication, we could build stronger, more resilient relationships that would pave the way for success and growth in the workplace.

I thought I would start by breaking it down for you!

The Traditionalists, The Silent Generation: *THE GOAT (The Greatest of All Time)*

The Traditionalist generation, also known as the Silent Generation, was born between 1928 and 1945. Yep, that's right, they're the OG grandmas and grandpas of the workplace. They grew up during the Great Depression, World War II, The Civil Rights movement, and the post-war economic boom. Basically, they've seen it all and lived through some major history-making moments.

During their upbringing, Traditionalists faced the challenges of a post-war society, including rationing, economic instability, and social change. Many of them entered the workforce at an early age, taking on jobs to help support their families. They experienced the introduction of television, the rise of rock and roll music, and the beginning of the space race. These events influenced their perspectives on technology, entertainment, and progress.

Nowadays, Traditionalists are often facing struggles in the workplace. Many of them are navigating the transition into retirement but may be hesitant because they may not be financially prepared to do so. They also often struggle with technology and the rapid pace of change in the modern workforce. They may feel undervalued and overlooked in favor of younger, more tech-savvy employees. Often seen as resistant to change, but really, they just value traditional ways of working and have a wealth of experience to offer. Additionally, they face age discrimination and difficulty finding opportunities for advancement, despite their years of experience and knowledge.

When it comes to other generations, Traditionalists tend to have mixed feelings. They may see Gen Xers as a bit rebellious and independent, but they also appreciate their pragmatism and resourcefulness. Millennials might be seen as overly focused on work-life balance, yet ambitious and innovative, but also impatient and entitled. Traditionalists do, however, admire their creativity and passion for making a difference. And as for Gen Z, well, they are likely viewed as mysterious and elusive creatures who seem to communicate solely through emojis. Traditionalists view them to be tech-savvy and socially conscious but lacking in traditional work ethic and respect for authority.

Traditionalists have seen some crazy things in their lifetime, and they're facing some legit challenges in the workplace. But hey, they've got their sense of humor and wisdom to get them through. And when it comes to the other generations, they probably just secretly want to be able to text as fast as a Gen Z-er without accidentally sending their boss a selfie. Do not count them out just yet – they may be silent, but they're still kicking butt and taking names in the office!

Baby Boomers:

Buckle up because we're about to take a trip back in time to when the Baby Boomers were coming of age. Picture this: it's the 1960s and the world is going through huge cultural and political changes *(hmmm sound familiar 2024?)*. The Civil Rights Movement is in full swing, the Vietnam War is causing widespread unrest, and the sexual revolution is challenging traditional norms. Baby Boomers were right in the middle of it all, grappling with these momentous events as they came of age.

They were raised by the generation that had lived through the Great Depression and valued hard work and responsibility with a strong emphasis on traditional values and discipline. This generation grew up in a time when children were expected to be seen and not heard, and there was a clear divide between the roles of men and women in the household. They saw the dawn of the television age, the rise of rock and roll music, and the emergence of the counterculture movement. It was a time of rebellion and social change, and boomers were right in the thick of it all. They were the generation that popularized the phrase "don't trust anyone over 30" and embraced the idea of "peace, love, and rock 'n roll."

This upbringing has certainly influenced how Baby Boomers approach work and life — they tend to value hard work, loyalty, and stability. They're not ones to jump from job to job or embrace change with open arms. They value stability and job security, which often translates into a preference for traditional 9-to-5 jobs, and they are the ones who will show up early and stay late until the job is done. And with this ingrained into their DNA, they often find it hard to understand the younger generations' desire for flexibility, work-life balance and clocking out at 5 on the dot *(and some even earlier).* They cringe at the statement, "why does it matter that I clocked in at 8:10 am, the work is still getting done!

As for their expectations of younger generations like the millennials and Gen Z, Baby Boomers often find themselves at odds with these up-and-comers. They may see them as entitled or lacking in work ethic, and struggle to understand their more casual approach to work and life. They also value loyalty and respect and may become frustrated with what they perceive as a lack of these qualities in the younger generations.

So, there you have it – a little insight into the world of Baby Boomers, where they are coming from and how they operate in the workplace. Remember, they may seem a bit set in their ways, but they've lived through some wild times and have a lot to offer in terms of wisdom and experience. And who knows, they might even crack a few great jokes along the way!

Gen X

Oh, Gen X, the forgotten middle child of generations born between the early 1960s and early 1980s. As a generation sandwiched between the Baby Boomers and Millennials, we often felt overlooked and overshadowed. This generation faced momentous events such as the Cold War, the rise of technology and the internet, an economic recession, the AIDS epidemic, and the threat of nuclear war. It is no wonder we have such a fighting spirit.

Our upbringing was a mix of tough love and independence. Many Gen Xers grew up in households affected by high rates of divorce, and often had to navigate shifting family dynamics and parental absence. Raised in a time when both parents were entering the workforce, Gen X were often referred to as the "latchkey kids", as they were left to fend for themselves after school while both parents were out working (*and I think we did surprisingly good*). This instilled in us a sense of self-reliance and independence.

During our formative years, noteworthy events were happening around the world that shaped our outlook on life. We witnessed the fall of the Berlin Wall (1989), the end of the Cold War, and the rise of grunge music. We grew up during a time of rapid social and cultural change *(see a pattern already),* and it definitely left a scar.

When it comes to work and life, Gen Xers are known for their work ethic and ability to juggle multiple responsibilities. We believe in putting in the hours and getting the job done, but we also value work-life balance and time for ourselves and our families. We are not afraid to speak our minds and push for change in the workplace, and our entrepreneurial spirit is strong. We're also known for our skepticism and distrust of authority.

In terms of what we expect from younger generations, we often find ourselves in a position of being both mentors and managers to Millennials and Gen Z. We expect the younger generations to be tech-savvy and adaptable, but we also hope to impart our wisdom and experience to them. We want to see the same level of resilience and independence. We also appreciate their fresh perspective and willingness to challenge the status quo but wish they would learn the art of timing *(just because they think it, we wish they wouldn't always say it out loud!)*. Learn from our mistakes.

So, while we may not always get the spotlight, Gen X is a generation that has faced significant challenges and has developed a unique approach to work and life. We bring a sense of realism and resourcefulness to the table, and we expect the same from the generations that follow. And hey, we do it all with a pretty killer sense of humor, too.

Millennials

Let's talk about Millennials, born between 1981 and 1996. These poor souls were growing up during some seriously tumultuous times. From the Y2K scare, the rise of technology and social media to the economic recession, Millennials were basically handed a big ole' bowl of uncertainty. I mean, can you imagine trying to plan for the future when the world economy is in the toilet and the internet is a battlefield of cat memes and political arguments? It's a wonder they made it out of their teenage years with their sanity intact.

Meanwhile, significant events around the world were shaping the lives of Millennials. We're talking about everything from 9/11 and the War on Terror to the global financial crisis. The rise of the internet and social media led to a greater sense of global awareness and interconnectedness. They were exposed to a wide range of information and ideas, leading to a more open-minded and inclusive worldview. It's no wonder Millennials have a little chip on their shoulder when it comes to things like job security and financial stability. They basically watched the world go up in flames while trying to figure out how to adult.

Now let's talk about how Millennials were raised. Helicopter parents, participation trophies, and the constant pressure to succeed in a rapidly changing world. Millennials were raised with a mix of grand expectations and constant coddling. They have been told they're special since day one, but they've also been pushed to excel in a world that doesn't always make it easy.

When it comes to work and life, Millennials are all about that work-life balance. They've seen their parents and older siblings grind themselves into the ground for the sake of their careers, and they're not about to make the same mistake. They want flexible work hours, remote options, and unlimited vacation time. And who can blame them? The world is a big, beautiful place, and Millennials want to see as much of it as possible.

As for what Millennials expect from younger and older generations, it all comes down to understanding and support. They want Gen Z to carry the torch of progressivism and social change. On the other hand, Millennials expect older generations like Gen X and Baby Boomers to be open to innovative ideas and new ways of working. They hope for understanding and support from older generations as they navigate their own challenges and strive for a better future.

Gen Z

Fellow, Gen X-ers and Baby Boomers, let me enlighten you on the struggles and events that shaped the minds of our beloved Generation Z (also known as the iGeneration, 1996-2012). Picture this: as they were growing up, they were bombarded with the rise of social media, the constant threat of climate change, and the aftermath of the 2008 fiscal crisis. No wonder they're always glued to their phones and advocating for sustainability! It's our fault because we are supposed to be grown-ups and raise them. We created this mess, yet we complain about it all the time.

Speaking of being raised, Gen Zs were the first generation to be raised in the digital age, with smartphones and tablets as their constant companions. Helicopter parenting was at its peak, with participation trophies and scheduled playdates being the norm. They were raised in a world that was increasingly interconnected, but also increasingly unpredictable. It's no wonder that they approach work and life with a mix of caution and boldness.

When it comes to work and life, Gen Z-ers are a whole new breed. They value flexibility and purpose in their careers, prioritizing work-life balance over climbing the corporate ladder, unlike their predecessors. This is particularly important to them, and we can all learn a thing or two from their mindfulness and focus on mental wellness.

Gen Z has some funny, but quite accurate observations about their older counterparts in the workplace. When it comes to Traditionalists and Baby Boomers, they see them as the OGs of the office, with their old-school work ethic, no-nonsense attitude, and tendency to use phrases like "back in my day." Gen Zs respect OG wisdom and experience and are happy to help them with their technology skills.

As for Gen X, they are seen as the cool aunts and uncles of the office. Gen Z appreciates their laid-back vibe and willingness to adapt to modern technology. Gen X might be the ones sneaking in a casual Friday dress code or suggesting a team happy hour, and Gen Z is here for it all! They might not always understand their obsession with '90s music and pop culture, but they admire their ability to casually drop movie quotes into a meeting.

As for the millennials, the big siblings of the office, Gen Z looks up to them for paving the way in changing workplace culture and valuing work-life balance. They appreciate their tech-savvy skills and their tendency to challenge traditional workplace norms. They might playfully tease their obsession with self-care and constant need for affirmation, but at the end of the day, they appreciate their progressive mindset.

Here's the kicker – despite Gen Z's laid-back approach to work, they are ambitious and crave opportunities for growth. And what do they expect from the older generations? Since they are not afraid to speak up, and they value diverse perspectives and are not afraid to challenge the status quo, as the older generations, we should mentor and guide them in their career paths. We have the privilege *(and huge undertaking)* to raise them up in our organizations, while also being open to learning from their fresh perspectives.

They may be obsessed with TikTok and avocado toast, but they are passionate, imaginative, and determined to make a difference in the world. After all, they are the future, and it looks like it's going to be bright and quite a ride.

Remember to approach this with no judgment of any generation and try to keep a sense of humor as you navigate through the differences in values and work styles. By embracing each generation's values and work styles, you will be on your way to building a cohesive and successful multi-generational team.

A Way Forward

In my professional experience, one incredibly helpful tool that can revolutionize a leader's management style in many ways is the understanding of generational differences. You can use it to gain a deeper understanding of how others communicate and connect with the five components of EQ (Emotional Intelligence). By understanding the unique individual's communication styles and work preferences, you can tailor your leadership approach to effectively connect with and lead any team.

Now that you've really worked diligently on improving your EQ, let's dive into the power of the DiSC. Grab a pen and paper, jot down your observations and reflections on this topic, and keep an open mind as you explore the values and motivations of each generation in your team.

In today's rapidly changing digital world of business, it is more crucial than ever for organizations to understand and adapt to the unique characteristics and communication styles of their team members. Integrating assessment tools like the DiSC into organizational practices can be a game-changer for companies.

As we navigate the effects of the 2020 pandemic and integrate the preferences of the next generation of workers, embracing assessment tools is not just a modern trend, but a necessary step in meeting the evolving needs of the workforce and staying ahead in a competitive market. But let's first debunk some false beliefs about assessments.

The Top 10 Misunderstandings About the Impact of the DiSC on Organizational Performance

- Embracing assessment tools like the DiSC will automatically guarantee organizational success. False

- The DiSC assessment is the only tool necessary for understanding and improving employee communication and collaboration. False

- Assessment tools like the DiSC can accurately predict employee performance and success in a role. False

- Investing in assessment tools like the DiSC will immediately lead to a more cohesive and productive team. Eventually!

- The results of the DiSC assessment are always accurate and reliable indicators of an individual's behavior and communication style. False

- Using the DiSC assessment will eliminate all conflicts and misunderstandings within the organization. False

- Organizational success hinges solely on the results of the DiSC assessment and does not require any other factors to be considered. False

- Assessment tools like the DiSC can accurately predict an individual's potential for leadership and managerial roles. False

- The use of the DiSC assessment will automatically lead to an increase in employee retention rates. False

- The results of the DiSC assessment can be used as the sole basis for employee promotions and advancement within the organization. False

Now that we got that out of the way, let's talk about the amazing benefits of this tool.

How a Single Activity Helped This Executive Bridge the Gap at Home and in the Workplace

I always considered it a privilege to be an executive coach, guiding successful individuals like Matt through their personal and professional journeys. One of the first steps in my coaching process is having my clients take the DiSC assessment, followed by deep conversations about their dreams, goals, values, and motivations. Every session is a new adventure, and I'm always surprised by the directions our conversations take us.

One day, I brought up the idea of creating a dream board with Matt. I could see the skepticism in his eyes, as if he thought this was a childish and irrelevant activity. "A dream board? Seriously Leoni, is this some sort of elementary art project to waste my time?"

Matt certainly did not hide his reluctance. He questioned the purpose of such an activity, dismissing it as "pie in the sky dream-like stuff." However, I encouraged him to try it, assuring him that there was value in visualizing his dreams and aspirations.

To my surprise, when Matt returned for our next session, he brought with him a strikingly colorful and elaborate dream board. I could not help but feel like a proud momma bear. It was clear that he had put considerable thought and effort into the project.

As he began to tell me about the details of his dream board, I could see a glimmer of excitement in his eyes. His face lit up as he described how, at first, he grumbled and complained about this homework assignment that he viewed as a silly project. However, his teenage daughters had overheard his conversation with his wife and eagerly offered to help him with his dream board.

It was a transformative experience for Matt and the family. Not only did his daughters eagerly pitch in and create their own dream boards, but for the first time in years, he spent quality time connecting with them. They laughed, bonded, and shared their hopes and dreams with each other. It was a beautiful moment of connection that Matt had longed for.

In that unexpected turn of events, Matt learned a valuable lesson. He realized the importance of prioritizing family time and rekindling the connections with his wife and daughters. As a result, their family dinners became more fun-filled with meaningful conversations. It was an activity that brought a heartwarming transformation that changed Matt's life forever.

In the end, the simple act of creating a dream board had unexpectedly rekindled the bond within his family, as Matt recalled, "it helped me communicate differently with my girls", and for that, Matt was eternally grateful. His wife and girls took the DiSC assessment as well and the impact was powerful. From that day forward, Matt made it his priority to connect and cherish the moments spent with his wife and daughters, creating a renewed sense of love and joy in their household.

P.S. Matt's wife ended up in my coaching program as she

wanted to rediscover her purpose after kids, and the girls are going through the program to discover their strengths and career paths.

*If you are interested in knowing YOUR DiSC Style, head to our website and use code: **BridgetheGap** for a discounted price.*

Unlocking Team Success: The Powerful Benefits of DiSC Assessment in the Workplace

- *Enhances communication* – The DiSC assessment helps employees understand their communication styles and how to effectively communicate with others in the workplace.

- *Improves teamwork* - The assessment helps individuals understand their roles in a team and how to work effectively with others who have different personalities and work styles.

- *Increases self-awareness* - Employees gain insight into their own behavior and how it impacts their work and the work of others.

- *Better conflict resolution* - Understanding different personality types and how they respond to conflict can lead to more effective conflict resolution in the workplace.

- *Increases productivity* - Employees are better able to

understand their strengths and weaknesses, leading to more efficient and effective work.

- *Enhances leadership development* - DiSC assessments can help identify individuals with leadership potential and provide insight into how to develop their leadership skills.

- *Improves customer relationships* - Understanding and adapting to different customer personalities can lead to better customer relationships and increased satisfaction.

- *Reduces turnover* - Employees who feel understood and supported are more likely to stay with an organization, reducing turnover.

- *Better decision-making* - Understanding different perspectives and work styles can lead to more well-rounded and informed decision-making.

- *More effective management* - Managers can use the DiSC assessment to better understand and communicate with their employees, leading to more effective management.

- *Increases employee engagement* - When employees feel understood and valued, they are more engaged in their work and the success of the organization.

- *Improves performance management* - The assessment can provide insight into how to effectively manage and motivate employees to improve their performance.

- *Better organizational culture* - DiSC assessments can lead to a more inclusivity and understanding organizational culture that values and respects different personalities and work styles.

Maybe you can relate to this next story.

The Key to Rebuilding a Toxic Team

I've had the opportunity to work with some of the most dysfunctional teams in organizations throughout my career. But let me tell you about one particular experience that truly stands out to me. I was called in to one of many branches of a global company. This was not the only branch on the verge of self-destruction due to toxic and dysfunctional work environments.

The conflicts within this branch were deeply rooted in the personalities, work styles, and values of the employees. There were generational gaps, misunderstandings, hurt feelings, and grudges festering for years. Previous toxic leadership had allowed this environment to thrive, and the new leader was facing a daunting challenge of initiating clean up on aisles 1,2,3 & 4. It was a mess!

I designed a 3-day workshop specifically for this organization, incorporating the use of one of my best tried and true tools, the DiSC assessment, as well as focusing on EQ and the dysfunctions of teamwork. The first day was spent building connections with the team, using the knowledge from their DiSC assessments to approach individuals in a way that resonated with them. Trust began to develop, and the healing process had begun.

As we delved into team exercises and conflict resolution, something incredible began to happen. During the second and third days, the breakthroughs were monumental. The team members started to forgive past grievances, understand each other's work styles, and break down the walls that had been erected for years. Silos between departments melted away, and relationships were rebuilt. It was a truly transformative experience, and the leaders were astonished at what had been achieved in just three days of raw, honest work.

To solidify the progress and promote ongoing growth, I created personalized DiSC profile cards for each team member, featuring "do's and don'ts" of communication based on their assessment. These cards were posted on their cubicles, fostering open and effective communication. The team embraced the exercise, letting their guard down and actively participating in the process of building a stronger, more united team.

The impact of this workshop transcended the three days we

spent together. Employees still reach out to share the continued positive influence of the program, sending pictures of their DiSC profile cards and how they were still guiding communication within the branch and how this translates to home life as well.

The most profound lesson that I and everyone in the team learned was the realization that we all bring something unique to the table. We all have different personalities, experiences, strengths, and unique perspectives that contribute to the success of our teams. It was undoubtedly the highlight of my career, and it has continued to inspire me to facilitate growth and positive change in teams.

"Leoni, one can never fully appreciate what you bring to improve people's development until they have spent time in your training sessions. I have been promoting you and your training program to our region to encourage everyone to have you in their branch this year! I love Tom's big takeaway he learned. He said that self-awareness is something we all need to be reminded of and for a couple of his team members this was their biggest takeaway as well. We get so busy and need to move on to the next task too quickly. Sometimes we don't prioritize our work relationships and they are so important. I am already seeing big changes in the way the team has improved in their communication with each other. Everyone is talking in "colored dots" and having fun with the learning they received from you. You sure are a unicorn at this company and

we are lucky to have snagged you when we did. We are looking forward to Leoni 2.0 ~ General Manager."

That's a wrap on the DiSC assessment and understanding each generation in the workplace. Take a moment to pat yourself on the back managing all that personality analysis and generational differences without pulling your hair out.

We've learned that just because Gary from accounting is a high C doesn't mean he's a total grump, and that Karen from marketing might be a bit of an I, but she's not just all talk, and no action.

Now, before you go off thinking you've got all the secrets to navigating the office, just remember that everyone is a unique blend of their personality type and generational influences. So, as much as we'd love to neatly categorize everyone into little boxes, it's important to remember that there's always more to each person than meets the eye.

No need to be overwhelmed with all this information because you don't have to do all the training and studying of assessments, you need to know who can help you and get it done!

Remember to embrace the diverse personalities and perspectives that each generation brings to the table. Let's laugh at the Baby Boomers' insistence on sending handwritten thank-you notes and the Millennials' obsession with avocado toast. Let's appreciate Gen Xers' ability to balance work and life and their tech-savvy skills.

And most importantly, let's keep learning from each other and finding ways to communicate and collaborate across the generational divide. Afterall, we are in this together, and a little humor and understanding can go a long way in building a happy and productive workplace.

Cheers!

Chapter 4:

From Suspicion to Solidarity: Growing Trust in a Multi-Generational Environment

This chapter will help you:

1. Understand the detrimental effects of dysfunctions of trust on a team and an organization, especially in a multi-generational environment.

2. Recognize the importance of trust as the cornerstone of strong relationships and a positive work environment and how it can bridge the gap between different generations in the workplace.

3. Identify examples of how trust can be broken in the workplace and how to take proactive steps to rebuild trust and restore positive relationships.

4. Advance your leadership skills by building trust with your team members from different generations, enhancing your ability to effectively communicate, inspire, and motivate your team.

5. Understand the benefits of a trust-filled team and a leader who can be trusted, leading to a cohesive and high-performing team, as well as loyalty, respect, and commitment among team members.

Let's keep the momentum going!

I don't know about you, but I am thrilled about all that you are learning through my experiences, training, education, and teaching! In this chapter, we will discuss the importance of building trust within a multi-generational workplace and how it can positively impact your leadership. Building trust is essential for leaders who want to cultivate a cohesive and high-performing team. Leaders who can bridge the gap of trust with employees from different generations can help their organizational bottom line by increasing employee retention and reducing employee costs.

Did you know, according to a 2024 Gallup report, 40% of employees say their jobs have a negative or extremely negative impact on their mental health.

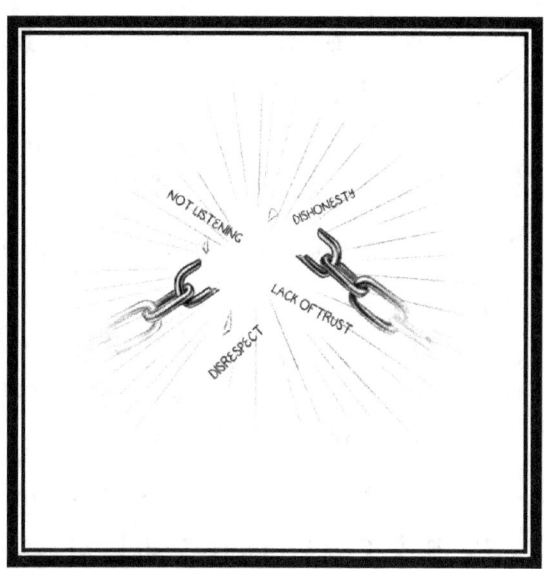

Figure 1. Trust is hard to earn, but easy to break. Trust links teams together.

Building a Dream Team with TRUST: How a Leader Inspired Growth and Triumph

I have always believed that the key to leading a successful team and to building trust quickly was through understanding your team members on a personal level. As the Director of Learning Development, I was given the privilege and challenge of leading a multi-generational team. This included members from Gen X, 3 Millennials, a Baby Boomer, and even

2 Gen Z's. It was a diverse and dynamic group, but it was also a group that posed a unique set of challenges.

At this point, I already knew each person's DiSC assessment results so one of the first things I did was to schedule one-on-one meetings with each team member, because I wanted to understand their individual strengths, weaknesses, dreams, and aspirations. I asked them about their job satisfaction, their leadership preferences, their communication preferences and where they saw themselves in the next one, two, and three years.

I also wanted to validate their contributions to the team and the organization thus far, and to hear more about their creative ideas for future innovations in L&D. My desire was for them to know that they were not just valuable to me, but vital to the success of the team and the organization.

During these meetings, I found that one of them was not entirely happy with her role. The dissatisfaction was undeniable, and it was affecting not only her attitude and demeanor but the overall dynamic of the team. It was clear that something needed to change.

Another team member was also feeling disheartened about her role but was unsure about her strengths and how to pivot. It was clear to me that by understanding their passions and strengths, I could create an opportunity to ignite their passion for their work again and give back that sense of meaning and value they once felt. Together, we rewrote their job description to align with those passions and strengths.

I didn't stop there. I encouraged all of them to take ownership of their growth and development. I asked them to find classes or training that would enhance their skill sets and benefit the team and the organization and after their feedback, I approved the requests for professional development, showing them that I was fully committed to their success and wellbeing.

The transformation in the team was nothing short of stunning. As they found joy and fulfillment in their work, they brought a new level of energy and dedication to the team. I witnessed a transformation in their attitudes and motivation. They were excited to come to work, they collaborated more effectively, and our productivity soared. It wasn't just about achieving individual happiness, but it was clear that our entire organization was benefiting from a team that was dynamic, skilled, and always striving for improvement.

I was humbled by their gratitude, by the tears of appreciation that they showed me. It wasn't about me - it was about them and their development. They felt seen, valued, and supported in a way they hadn't experienced before.

Through this experience, I learned that true leadership is built on the foundation of TRUST. It is not about me, but about empowering and inspiring others to reach their goals and their growth potential. When I chose to say yes to a leadership role, I wholeheartedly committed to supporting my team's professional growth and development.

In the end, I have come to realize that when you put others first, when you value their strengths and passions, the possibilities are endless. The triumph of the human spirit was on clear display within my team, and it has left a lasting impact on me as a leader. Their growth sparked a fire within me, and I am excited to continue inspiring and empowering others in their journey to success.

"Leoni, words cannot express my sadness that you are no longer my boss. Your team, we had a front row seat to the incredible impact and influence you had on everyone. You were the greatest leader I ever worked for and the fact that you graciously provided hard feedback and relentlessly coached me and believed in me. No one could ever have done it with so much class as you. You believed in me more than even my own family and you saved me, and I am forever grateful. Life and work will not be the same without you! ~Sarah"

The Effects of Dysfunctions of Trust on a Team and in an Organization:

Dysfunctions of trust can have a detrimental impact on a team and an organization. When trust is lacking, communication breaks down, collaboration becomes difficult, and productivity suffers. In a multi-generational environment, distrust can lead to conflict between different age groups, hindering the smooth functioning of the team. As a leader, it is essential to recognize the signs of trust dysfunctions and address them promptly to create a cohesive and high-performing team.

Why Trust is Important:

If your employees do not trust their leader or their organization, the employees who are burned out are 63% more likely to not show up (quiet quitting) and 2X as likely to be looking for a new job. ~ Gallup Report

---

Trust is the cornerstone of strong relationships, both in the workplace and beyond. Lack of trust within a team or organization can lead to decreased productivity, lack of collaboration, and a toxic work environment. Additionally, lack of trust can lead to higher turnover rates, as employees may feel undervalued and unsupported. Have you ever worked for or know someone who complains of distrusting leaders or organizations? Are you or your organization guilty of any of the following?

Distrust and Disengagement: 14 Examples of Distrustful Behaviors to Avoid

- *Micromanaging:* Constantly checking in on employees

and questioning their every move, demonstrating a lack of trust and confidence in their abilities.

- *Refusal to delegate tasks:* Taking on all responsibilities themselves, unwilling to share the workload with the team due to a lack of trust in the work will get done right.

- *Monitoring communication:* Keeping a close eye on all employee interactions, such as emails and meetings, time spent chatting at someone's desk, indicating a lack of trust in their team's professionalism.

- *Lack of transparency:* Withholding valuable information and decision-making processes from employees, demonstrating a lack of trust in their ability to handle challenging or sensitive information.

- *Blaming rather than coaching:* Pointing fingers at employees for mistakes instead of providing constructive feedback and guidance, displaying a lack of trust in their employees' ability to learn and grow from their errors.

- *Questioning decision-making:* Second-guessing and challenging the choices made by employees, indicating a lack of trust in their judgment and decision-making skills.

- *Disregarding input:* Ignoring or dismissing suggestions

and ideas from employees, showing a lack of trust in their creativity and problem-solving abilities.

- *Inflexibility:* Refusing to entertain alternative approaches and solutions put forward by employees, indicating a lack of trust in their competency to think outside-the-box.

- *Undermining authority:* Interfering with employees' interactions with other team members and higher-ups, highlighting a lack of trust in their employees' ability to manage professional relationships effectively.

- *Excessive monitoring:* Implementing strict surveillance measures and constant performance evaluations, checking their badging in and out, demonstrating a lack of trust in their employees' work ethic and dedication.

- *Lack of autonomy:* Imposing stringent rules and regulations that limit employees' freedom to make independent decisions, displaying a lack of trust in their ability to act responsibly without constant supervision.

- *Public criticism:* Calling out employees for their mistakes in front of their colleagues, demonstrating a lack of trust in their employees' competence and professionalism.

- *Withholding opportunities for growth:* Failing to provide training and advancement opportunities, indicating a lack of trust in their employees' ability to take on new challenges and responsibilities.

- *Fostering a culture of fear:* Creating an environment where employees are hesitant to take risks or be innovative, showcasing a lack of trust in their ability to contribute positively to the organization.

When trust is broken in the workplace, it can have a significant impact on both the team and the organization. Let's explore examples of the implications of broken trust in the workplace and how they can affect the overall dynamics and success of the team and organization.

The Cost of Distrust: The 15 Implications of Broken Trust in the Workplace

- Lack of communication

- Reduced collaboration

- Decreased productivity.

- Increase in conflict.

- Low morale

- Difficulty in problem-solving

- Decreased employee engagement.

- Decreased loyalty.

- Increased turnover

- Negative effects on employee mental health

- Erosion to the company culture

- Reduced effectiveness of team meetings

- Decreased job satisfaction.

- Loss of company reputation

- Negative impact on overall organizational performance

Here's the good news!

Trust fosters a positive work environment where individuals feel valued and appreciated. In a multi-generational setting, trust bridges the gap between different age groups, allowing for better understanding and collaboration. Without trust, your leadership skills are about as effective as a chocolate teapot - *sweet, but useless.*

As a trusted and respected leader, the positive benefits of building outstanding trust relationships with the team and the organization cannot be overstated. From improved employee morale and productivity to enhanced team cohesion and collaboration, the impact of a strong leader who prioritizes trust and respect is truly remarkable.

 Watch this 3:48 minute video
https://www.youtube.com/watch?v=MAfGb-AYx6l&ab_channel=SimonSinek

Let's highlight the amazing benefits when trust exists!

The Power of Trust: A List for Successful Leadership

- *Increased morale and motivation* - when employees feel valued and supported by a trusted leader, they are more likely to feel motivated to perform at their best.

- *Enhanced teamwork and collaboration* - a leader who has built outstanding trust relationships with the team can foster a sense of unity and collaboration among team members, leading to improved productivity and innovation.

- *Higher employee retention* - when employees trust their leader and feel a sense of loyalty to the organization, they are more likely to stay with the company long-term, reducing turnover and associated costs.

- *Improved communication* - a trusted leader can create an environment of open and transparent communication, allowing for better information sharing and understanding among team members.

- *Increased job satisfaction* - when employees feel

supported and trusted by their leader, they are more likely to experience job satisfaction and overall happiness in their work. And for the record, this also leads to a happier home life.

- *Greater employee engagement* - a trusted leader can inspire and engage employees in their work, leading to a more committed and resolute workforce.

- *Better decision-making* - a leader who has built outstanding trust relationships with the team can foster an environment where team members feel comfortable sharing their input, leading to more informed and effective decision-making.

- *Increased loyalty and commitment* - employees who trust their leader are more likely to feel a sense of loyalty and commitment to the organization, leading to better performance and dedication.

- *Reduced stress and conflict* - a trusted leader can help create a positive and supportive work environment, reducing stress and minimizing conflicts among team members.

- *Enhanced innovation and creativity* - a leader who fosters trust and respect can encourage creativity and innovation among team members, leading to innovative ideas and solutions.

- *Better customer satisfaction* - when employees feel supported and trusted by their leader, they are more likely to provide better service to customers, leading to increased customer satisfaction.

- *Enhanced company culture* - a trusted leader can help shape a positive and inclusive company culture.

- *Improved overall performance* - when a leader has built outstanding trust relationships with the team, the organization is more likely to experience improved overall performance and success.

How Trust Will Advance Your Leadership Skills

As a leader, earning the trust of your team members is like planting the seeds of professional growth. Without trust, you are just a leader in title, not in practice. Your team will not follow you willingly, and you will spend most of your time herding cats instead of leading a motivated, cohesive group. When your team trusts you, they will have your back, respect your decisions, and be willing to go the extra mile. It was John Maxwell who once said, "A leader has followers, otherwise he/she is just taking a walk." In short, trust is the secret sauce that makes great leaders great!

Trust enhances your credibility and influence, making it easier to motivate and inspire others. It's like having a secret superpower that allows you to lead without having to constantly prove yourself. Your team will be more likely to believe in your vision and work towards common goals. Plus, when trust is present, your words carry more weight, and you can positively influence the attitudes and behaviors of those around you.

In a multi-generational environment, being a trusted leader allows you to bridge generational gaps and create a thriving work culture. Whether you are managing Traditionalists, Baby Boomers, Gen X, Millennials, or Gen Z, trust is the common denominator that transcends age and creates a sense of unity. When your team members from different generations trust you, they will be more open-minded, willing to collaborate, and learn from one another. It's like being the DJ at a family reunion, blending the oldies with the latest hits to keep everyone on the dance floor.

So, how do you gauge if trust is present in your team and organization? Look for signs of open communication, mutual respect, and a willingness to take risks and be vulnerable. Trustworthiness is hard to measure, it cannot be measured on a spreadsheet, but you will know it when you see it. If your team members feel comfortable sharing their ideas, giving you and others feedback, and will share their dreams and goals, then there is a good chance you're nailing it!

Bridging the Gap: "The Ultimate Trust-Building Toolkit"

- Conduct a personality assessment for each team

member to better understand their strengths, weaknesses, and communication styles.

- Schedule regular one-on-one meetings with team members to discuss their career goals and aspirations.

- Implement mentorship programs for younger team members to learn from more experienced colleagues and vice versa (reverse mentoring).

- Encourage team bonding activities such as team building workshops, volunteering activities, or group outings to foster trust and camaraderie and ask each generation for their feedback and ideas.

- Create a feedback culture where team members feel comfortable giving and receiving constructive criticism.

- Provide opportunities for cross-generational knowledge sharing through workshops, presentations, or job shadowing.

- Develop a clear set of values and principles for the team to align on, emphasizing the importance of trust and collaboration.

- Recognize and celebrate individual and team achievements to boost morale and build trust.

- Invest in leadership development programs for both

junior and senior team members to improve their understanding of trust building activities.

- Encourage a culture of continuous learning and improvement, where team members are empowered to take initiative and develop their skills.

- Implement flexible work arrangements to accommodate the needs and preferences of different generations within the team.

- Lead by example by exhibiting trustworthiness, empathy, and respect for all team members, regardless of their age or background.

Remember, trust is the key to unlocking the full potential of your multi-generational team.

Take a deep breath!

Now take a few minutes to answer these questions:

- What will you start implementing immediately? Why?

_____

_____

_____

_____

_____

_____

_____

- How will you measure your success?

_____

_____

_____

_____

_____

_____

Chapter 5.

The Power of Coaching: Unleashing the Power of Multi-Generational Development and Growth

As a certified coach, I/O psychology scholar, and lover of all things related to people development, I am so excited about this chapter! We will explore the significant role of coaching in leading multi-generational teams (friends and family members) and how it can be a powerful tool for unleashing the potential of your employees from different generations.

This chapter will help you:

1. Understand the significant role of coaching in leading

multi-generational teams.

2. Learn the difference between managing and coaching and why coaching is essential for developing team members.

3. Create a culture of continuous learning and growth within your organization.

4. Recognize the benefits of coaching, including increased engagement, motivation, and performance among team members.

5. Overcome common barriers to coaching and implement strategies for coaching for performance to create a high-performing team.

My Personal Story and Why I am Passionate About Coaching

I was in my early thirties when I decided to start my real estate business. Moving to a brand-new state with my husband and three young toddlers, I had no idea where to start. At this time, I had a background in nursing, retail management, B2B sales, and years in cosmetology. It was a time of uncertainty, but I was determined to start a real estate business in this new place, despite not knowing anybody. I had to work, but I also wanted to be available to my kids.

I joined Keller Williams, a well-known real estate company, because they offered a lot of training and development. I took all the classes, soaked in all the knowledge, did everything they told me to do to learn how to run a successful real estate business. I networked, prospected, cold called, and I sat in coffee shops, nail salons, waiting rooms and more, eager to make connections. I was armed with a name tag, my business cards, and a hunger for success.

But after the first year, I only had one closing. I was starting to doubt myself and my abilities. It was then that a fellow realtor suggested I attend a real estate conference where I learned about the benefits of getting a career coach. At first, I was hesitant. I thought, "Why would I pay somebody all this money to tell me what to do when I already know what I need to do? It was a significant investment, but my husband supported me and encouraged me to try something different.

I decided to take the leap and get a coach. Little did I know that this decision would change my life in ways I could never have imagined. My coach helped me understand myself on a deeper level. It was then when I found out I was a dominant/influencing personality DiSC style, a go-getter personality (DI – red/yellow).

My coach pointed out that my dominant personality and my drive to always win were holding me back. I was always in fight or flight mode, clawing my way to be seen, heard, and respected, especially as an immigrant. I had always vowed never to let anyone make me feel less than because I was different. It was a realization that left me stunned and opened my eyes to the barriers I had placed on my own path to success.

Having a coach was a life-changing experience. It took me from good to great. I am a believer in Jesus Christ and when I say I love the Lord, baby, that is an understatement because I wouldn't be here today (that's for another book)! Nonetheless, I always had a fantastic support system, but this coach was my reality check! *I was the barrier to my success!* I did not fully believe that I belonged in success or in the circles of successful people because of my background. I didn't even know how I defined success. My coach helped me break through those self-imposed limitations. *Then, we got to work!*

The impact of coaching was profound. It transformed my life and my mindset. I realized the power of coaching in helping individuals reach their full potential. I fully embraced the person I always was, compassionate, loving, kind, with a slight hint of hood and fight!

This transformational journey ignited a fire within me, and I am incredibly passionate about leaders learning to coach their teams and employees. I have come to understand the profound impact coaching can have on individuals - lifting them up, empowering them, and helping them dream, believe in themselves, and experience breakthroughs. Great leaders who coach their employees can profoundly change lives, the impact resonating for generations to come.

What is Coaching?

Coaching is a development tool that involves guiding and supporting individuals to reach their full potential. As a leader, it involves asking thought-provoking questions, providing constructive feedback, and helping team members set and achieve their goals. Unlike managing, which focuses on directing and controlling tasks, coaching is about empowering and developing people. The coaching practice is a skill of curiosity and effective listening. It' helps you ignite inspiration to move someone forward to achieve exceptional results.

The biggest communication problem leaders encounter is that they do not listen to understand, they listen to reply.
~Franklin Covey

For example, instead of simply telling a team member how to complete a project, a coach would ask open-ended questions to help them identify their own solutions and strategies. Open-ended questions that encourage reflection and exploration, such as "What do you think is the best approach to tackling this challenge?" or "What obstacles do you foresee and how can you overcome them?" can prompt deep thinking and self-discovery.

So, picture this: a leader, Bob, walks up to an employee and says,

"Hey, I've got this project for you. It's a doozy, but I know you can handle it."

The employee, being the eager beaver they are, responds with, *"Great! But, uh, how do I even start?"*

Bob goes into coaching mode with an **exploratory question:**

What do you already know about this project?

What have you done in the past that has worked well?

What approach do you think would be best?

Then Bob goes into **action questions**:

What do you think is the first step?

What resources do you think you might need?

How can you break down the project into manageable tasks?

Who can help you right now?

Fast forward a bit and the employee hits a roadblock. They come back to the leader, looking as if they are about to pull their hair out. The leader, ever the helpful coach, doesn't just swoop in and save the day. Instead, they start firing off **empowering questions** like:

What options do you have right now to overcome this obstacle?

What have you learned from similar situations in the past?

What strengths can you tap into to find a solution?

What's one small step you can take to move forward?

What else?

What else?

What else? (yes, that was 3 times)

What's the worst that could happen if you try something new?

And just when you think it's all over, Bob and the employee jump into a mind mapping frenzy! It's like unleashing a brainstorming hurricane, letting ideas flow like a river in spring. They plot out different paths, connect the dots, and boom, the project starts to take shape.

Bob nudges the employee to think outside the box, explore new perspectives, and consider different angles. You're not just giving the employee a fish – you are teaching them how to fish (metaphorically speaking, of course).

Defining the Difference Between Managing and Coaching

Managing is essential for overseeing day-to-day tasks and ensuring work is completed efficiently. Managing involves directing and controlling the work of your team members. On the other hand, coaching focuses on developing the skills, knowledge, and potential of team members. Coaching focuses on empowering and developing employees. As a leader, *you need to strike a balance between managing and coaching to build a high-performing team.*

For example, instead of saying, "Why did you make that mistake?" Consider asking, "What do you think went wrong, and how can we prevent it in the future?"

Do you see the difference? It is quite profound when you implement a coaching style! Now if you have not approached things this way in the past, don't look crazy to your team and implement everything in one day. Be subtle, small adjustments, organic change. This is an evolution in your leadership style not a revolution.

Better yet just be honest with them and tell them you are learning something new and would like to try a better approach to leading. This demonstrates to your team that you are open-minded and ready to learn.

The Importance of the Sequence of Questioning

As a leader, it is important to take a coaching approach with your employees because let's face it, no one wants a boss who just barks orders and doesn't give a rip about their personal development. This coaching approach shows that you care about your employees' growth and success. It shows that you value their input and are committed to helping them reach their full potential and it helps to build a more positive and collaborative workplace culture. Think of it as you are the Mr. Miyagi to the Karate Kid (yep totally aged myself, but that's okay because the remake 2024 will bring Gen Z all up to speed!). Your people will win when they follow your intentional coaching. And you win when they win because leaders eat last! (another great read by Simon Sinek).

Now, let's talk about the proper sequencing of coaching questions. It's like baking a cake but throwing all the ingredients in a pan, sticking it in the oven and hoping for the best- you're just going to end up with a hot mess, my friend. You need to follow a specific recipe to create something delicious. It is all about guiding them through a logical thought process to help them reach their "aha" moment.

Here's a little example to drive home the importance of proper sequencing. So, let's say one of your employees is struggling with time management (seems to be most employees are struggling with this nowadays). You can't just start bombarding them with questions like, "Why can't you manage your time better?" That's like you trying to assemble a piece of furniture from a certain Swedish retailer known for its meatballs and minimalist designs. If you start by asking, "How do we attach the legs?" before you've even opened the box, well, you're in for a world of confusion. But if you start with, "Where's the instruction manual?" followed by, "What's the first step?" and then progress to, "How do we secure the legs?", we know the outcome is less frustrating and marriages stay intact!

This is the same idea as coaching. You start with a broad question like, "What aspects of your job do you find most challenging to manage?" Then, you would move on to more specific questions like, "What specific tasks or distractions are eating up most of your time?" See, it's all about that logical flow of questions to help them uncover the root of the issue and come up with a plan to tackle it.

For instance, when coaching a team member on a project, you might start by asking, "What are the different ways we can approach this project?" and then transition to, "What specific steps can you take to move this project forward?"

Now it's your turn to try this technique!

What are the Key Benefits of Coaching for Leaders?

Leading a multi-generational team can be complex, but taking on a coaching approach can bring countless benefits to both the team and the leader. By leveraging the strengths of different generations and fostering a culture of continuous learning and growth, leaders can effectively engage and motivate their team members while also driving innovation and collaboration.

- *Increased collaboration:* Coaching encourages team members of all generations to work together, leading to better collaboration and problem-solving.

- *Enhanced communication:* Coaching helps improve communication across different age groups by promoting active listening and open dialogue.

- *Bridging the generation gap*: Taking on the coaching approach helps bridge the generation gap by promoting understanding and empathy between team members.

- *Knowledge sharing:* Coaching encourages the sharing of knowledge and skills between different generations, leading to a more well-rounded team.

- *Increased motivation:* Coaching can help increase motivation within a multi-generational team by recognizing and leveraging the strengths of each generation.

- *Reduced conflict:* Coaching promotes understanding and empathy, which can help reduce conflict within a multi-generational team.

- *Mentoring opportunities:* Coaching provides opportunities for mentorship between team members of different generations, leading to valuable learning experiences.

- *Overall team success:* By taking on the coaching

approach, a multi-generational team can experience overall success by leveraging the unique strengths and perspectives of each generation.

Leading with Impact: A List for Overcoming Generational Barriers in Coaching

- *Resistance to change:* Team members may be resistant to the coaching approach due to established habits and familiarity with their current leadership style.

- *Generational stereotypes*: People may hold onto negative stereotypes about other generations, preventing them from fully engaging in a coaching approach.

- *Lack of understanding:* Some team members may not fully understand the benefits and principles of coaching, leading to skepticism, resistance, and inaction.

- *Power dynamics:* Hierarchical power dynamics can make it difficult for coaching to be effectively implemented, especially if older generations are resistant to being coached by younger leaders.

- *Resistance from senior management:* Senior management may be resistant to change and may not support the adoption of a coaching approach with a multi-generational team. I believe this evolution in your approach yields results when you don't ask permission, but forgiveness! *(there will be no need for that because it is a bullet-proof approach!)*

- *Different learning styles:* Different generations may have different learning preferences, making it challenging to find a coaching approach that resonates with everyone.

- *Time constraints:* This one is the hardest hurdle to overcome. **YES!** It takes time to coach, but it saves money and time in the long run. It took you how long to learn the habits of bad managing? Only because you were promoted with ZERO guidance on how to be an effective leader.

- *Fear of failure*: Some team members may fear failure or making mistakes in a coaching environment, leading them to resist the approach. And your fear of rejection is a good place to start. Why? Because you do care about your people.

- *Lack of skills:* Leaders and team members may lack the necessary coaching skills, leading to a barrier in effectively implementing the approach. That is why you are reading this book.

- *Fear of losing control:* Some leaders may fear losing control or authority by embracing a coaching approach, leading to resistance.

- *Resistance to feedback:* Team members may resist the idea of receiving feedback from colleagues, particularly from younger or less experienced leaders. Why? Because feedback has a negative rap! Your job as a leader is to reinvent the word *"feedforward."*

- *Organizational culture:* The existing organizational culture may not align with the principles of coaching, making it difficult to fully embrace the approach.

- *Lack of trust:* A lack of trust between team members of different generations can create a barrier to effective coaching and collaboration. You are ahead of the game at this point because you already decided to build trust with your team from the last chapter!

To be successful at anything, you do not have to be brilliant or unique. You simply need to do what most people are not doing...Be Consistent and Determined!

COACHING is a powerful tool for unleashing the potential of multi-generational teams. Coaching is a long game. Be a catalyst for your teams' transformational growth. Be the pace setter in your organization as a leader coach. Keep up the great work and stay tuned for the next chapter where we will delve into another essential aspect of multi-generational leadership.

Cheers!

Resources

There are various coaching resources and tools available to help leaders effectively coach their multi-generational teams. These may include:

- Coaching workshops for you as a leader

- Online courses, about coaching models and frameworks

- Excellent books

- LMS – learning management system for your organization

- Team building workshops for your team.

- Mentorship programs – if you do not have one, empower someone on your team to spearhead a program.

- Create an environment for cross-functional team projects for knowledge sharing.

- Recognitions programs for all ages and levels of work outputs

If you are interested in my 100+ FREE Coaching Questions, head over to my website to download!

Chapter 6.

Radical Respect: Leading Multi-Generational Teams with Heart and Humor

This chapter will help you:

1. Understand the importance of navigating your own opinions while honoring everyone else's individuality and perspectives.

2. Learn to understand the effects of demanding conformity from your multi-generational team.

3. Understand what it truly means to respect everyone, even the person whom you think can do nothing for

you at the time.

4. Learn the importance of transparency and open, honest communication and join the rest of the team.

I want to take a moment to applaud you for coming this far and investing in you, your team, and your organization. I also want to take this opportunity to acknowledge that it is not easy to throw everything you've known that has worked out the window including the baby and the bath water. It may be that you just need to make a few minor adjustments and implement a couple of new strategies, or you really do need to reimagine everything about being an effective leader that will stand the test of time! Only you can answer that question, but I am here to help you!

Let's dive into this final chapter!

A Personal Story of Command and Control to Respect and Understanding

This is a very personal story that I hope will resonate with leaders who are struggling to connect and lead multi generations in the workplace or even at home. I believe it carries a powerful message of the life-changing effects that respect, and understanding can produce.

I am a mother to three biological children, who are now young adults. Almost seven years ago now, the Lord called our family to open our home and hearts to two young teenagers, a brother and sister, aged 14 and 15 at the time. Their parents had abandoned them; their father, incarcerated, and mother was a drug addict. These two teenagers attended my kids' school, but certainly didn't run in the same circles. They came from a background of emotional and physical abuse, rejection, and abandonment. In contrast, our own children were raised with love, nurturing, provision, and care.

The personality and communication conflicts were 10X greater with five teenagers as opposed to three. Jeff and I quickly realized we were outnumbered and had to find a way to effectively bridge the gap between our own children, who were trying to find their way in the world and these two teenagers who had experienced immense trauma and now trying to pick up the pieces and find their value. This was a complex task that we had to navigate very carefully. As we tried to integrate these two young people into our family, while also maintaining a strong connection with our own children, it was evident we needed lots of prayers and a new approach!

One specific incident took place with my 15-year-old son, who was fighting to cut the cord from me because he was trying to man up! We were always remarkably close, but those years from 15-18 were rocky. Why? Because I was being close-minded to the way I thought I had to parent him. Tough love is great, but not when it kills someone's spirit. I found myself using the same parenting techniques I had used when he was younger - techniques of command and control, conditional demands, and threats. But it was no longer effective. It was damaging our relationship.

I decided to take a page out of my own book and change my approach. I figured what the heck do I have to lose (wait a lot... a relationship with my son). If these fundamental principles work on people in my coaching practice, then I should try it on my kids. As a certified Behavioral Analyst in the DiSC assessment tool, I decided to have all the children take it and the results were eye-opening.

As mentioned before, my DiSC personality style was ID (influence/dominant). I was incredibly dominant, high-intensity, and extroverted, and I wanted things done quickly, efficiently, and my way. When I get excited about what I am passionate about, I use big hand motions and I am extremely animated. *In contrast,* my son's DiSC personality was a solid S - steady and dependable, introverted and calm. We were complete opposites on the spectrum. This revelation opened my eyes to the challenges we were facing in communication and understanding each other.

I learned to be mindful of my blind spots and understand how my son wanted to be treated and communicated with. I needed to be more chill, speak to him in a softer voice, ask him for his opinion (instead of telling him what it should be), and I needed to show him more respect by honoring his communication style. An S's greatest fear is loss of security. My love and our home are his security and when I would raise my voice and show disappointment, it would crush him, and he would shut down. This revelation required a significant shift in my approach to parenting.

I learned to respect my son, his opinions, and his perspective (and trust me, there were times when I really questioned his sanity, LOL). Fast forward now at 22 years of age, I recognized his brilliance and maturity, and I enjoy my conversations with him because I am always learning from him. Our relationship transformed, and today, my son and I share a deep and meaningful bond. I credit this transformation to my willingness to reflect on myself, my emotional intelligence, and my blind spots.

In conclusion, I have learned that in leading a family, a team, or any group of individuals, it is essential to take the time to understand each person's unique needs, motivations, perspectives, and communication styles. By acknowledging our own blind spots and constantly working on our emotional intelligence, we can build strong, trusting relationships that lead to success and mutual respect. The power of respect and understanding cannot be underestimated, and when we take the time to truly listen and connect with those around us, we pave the way for growth, unity, and meaningful change.

My hope is that by sharing my story, I can inspire and encourage other leaders to embrace the power of respect and understanding, and build stronger, more cohesive teams and families, where every individual feels valued, heard, and appreciated.

As a leader, your job is to build the people and the people will build the business.

Corporate Betrayal: How Insecure Leaders Are Fueling Employee Disillusionment

I have heard so many of my coaching clients looking to be promoted to leadership ranks express their frustration with their bosses and the lack of trustworthiness they feel in their workplace. It is unbelievable to me that finding a leader you can trust is becoming increasingly difficult in America. The conflicts we coach through revolve around my clients being told how amazing they are by their bosses, only to have their ideas and strategies taken and shared by their superiors without proper credit or acknowledgment. Why is this a thing in corporate America? What is this backstabbing all about? Why are some leaders so insecure?

One client shared with me how she would have all these amazing ideas, brainstorm with her boss, and be told what an awesome impact she was making, only to have her boss take credit for her ideas and present them as his own to the president/CEO and other decision-makers of the organization. This happened on several occasions and left my client feeling defeated, undervalued, and always suspicious of her boss.

BTW, the sign of a bad leader or colleague in general, is if they don't bring your name up in the rooms you are not in!

As a trainer, consultant, and coach in these corporate companies, this behavior does not surprise me anymore. I have come to realize that leaders who behave in this manner are insecure, lack trust, and are willing to take credit for the hard work and ideas of their subordinates. They tend to take your ideas and share them as their own, leading initiatives as if they were their own creation.

The conclusion I have come to is that these types of leaders are dangerous for any organization. Their insecurities, lack of trustworthiness, jealousy and backstabbing behavior create disengagement and disloyalty among employees, leaders, and the organizational culture. This toxic behavior is driving the younger generations away, as they are witnessing these actions and are refusing to be a part of such negative, toxic work environments. These younger generations value work-life balance, and this kind of behavior is off balance to them.

The cautionary lesson in this story is clear - be wary of leaders who lack trust, who are manipulative, canning with their words, and take credit for the work of others. These leaders are toxic and will ultimately drive away the employees they so desperately want to recruit and retain.

It is a lesson in the importance of integrity, trust, and true leadership. Be the change that you know your organization needs. Be the leader you wish you had when you were starting your career journey. These younger generations are looking for strong leadership!

Honoring Other's Individuality and Contributions

We are all different, and that's what makes life interesting! So why should we expect our team members to be exactly like us? Embrace the diversity of thoughts, ideas, and values within your team. Take the time to appreciate the individuality of each team member. Celebrate the things that make them unique, whether it's their quirky sense of humor, their unconventional approach to problem-solving, or their love of pineapple on pizza (hey, to each their own). Who knows, maybe we'll learn a thing or two! Let's get ready to embrace some new ideas, instead of stubbornly clinging to our own way of doing things. Be open to different approaches and be willing to adapt and grow.

Also, we do not have to parent the younger team members: Look, we are not here to be helicopter managers, hovering over our younger team members and telling them how to do everything. Instead, we should treat them like the grown-up, capable colleagues that they are. Sure, they might not have as much experience as us, they may not be the best at navigating corporate "norms" yet, but they still deserve to be treated with respect.

Empower them by taking a mentoring and coaching approach, offering guidance and support without being overly directive. Trust me, they will appreciate being treated like equals.

My Worth IS NON-NEGOTIABLE!

I have had some incredible experiences in my life and my career, but one that truly stands out is the time I made a drastic career change for the sake of my children's education. It all started when the president of a university called me into his office after hearing about me from my daughter, who was a first-year student at the time. After spending an hour in his office getting to know each other, he offered me a job. This job would cover the cost of college tuition for all my children (and I ended up obtaining a master's degree as well). With five teenagers, two of whom were heading to college, and two following the next year, it was an offer I couldn't refuse.

I left my dream job at American Airlines to take this position, even though it was several steps down from where I was in my corporate career. I became a dean's administrative assistant – a role that was humble, to say the least. The Dean I worked for was old school, a micromanager (so comical that he would check the number of pencils and pens I went through per week lol), and he was incredibly disrespectful and demeaning. It was a far cry from the respect and understanding I had come to expect and give in my professional life.

However, there was a pivotal moment that turned things around for me. It was when my boss, the very same man who had been treating me poorly, suggested that I read a book called *'The Fred Factor.'* It was meant as a dig because he did not think I was humble enough and thankful enough for this opportunity. It was a great recommendation and a wonderful reminder of how I should approach everything in life, specifically my work.

And that's when everything changed. I sent the president an email stating that I valued my worth and that I would never treat anyone like this man was treating me. I rendered my resignation. *My worth is NOT NEGOTIABLE!*

Within 24 hours, I was introduced to a new Dean, and he turned out to be the BEST boss I have ever had in my career thus far. He was empowering, inspiring, and simply amazing. Working under his leadership was a game-changer. He treated me with profound respect, and he made it clear that I was a valued member of the team. He honored my perspective, innovative approach to business, and he loved my spunk! I am where I am today because somebody chose to see my strengths and my talents. In addition, he talked about me in the rooms that I could not speak for myself. This is how I became the Director of Career Development just seven months later. And that is the kind of leader I will follow!

And might I add, he was old enough to be my father, but was the most open-minded Boomer ever!

This experience taught me the power of resilience, the importance of standing up for oneself, and the impact that respect and understanding can have on a person's life. I learned that no matter how tough the circumstances may be, there is always a way to rise above them. Dr. D's leadership style showed me that it is possible to build a positive work environment where everyone feels valued and empowered.

So, to all the leaders out there struggling to connect and lead different generations in the workplace, I want you to understand the life-changing effects that respect, honor, and understanding can produce. It is not just about professional success; it's about creating an environment where everyone can thrive.

Respect Everyone, Regardless of Position

Respect should be given to everyone in the workplace, regardless of their position or title. This includes everyone from the janitor, mailperson, and the receptionist to the CEO and every member of your team. Every person plays a vital role in the organization, and demonstrating respect for all individuals fosters a culture of appreciation, inclusivity, and kindness. There is nothing that angers me more than watching leaders dismiss and disrespect employees. It happens daily and we need to be better!

Workplace Respect: The Life-Changing Effects of Honoring Every Individual

I have always made it a priority to connect with and invest in the people I work with, no matter their position or background. I passionately believe that respect and understanding can have life-changing effects, and I strive to embody these values in all my interactions. I am certainly not perfect, because I have been known to apologize for my harsh responses at times.

Two encounters with women janitors stand out vividly in my memory. Every time I saw them, I made it a point to stop and chat with them about their families and past experiences, their weekends and even their dreams and goals in life and work. I made it my mission to thank them for their hard work and dedication every day.

One of the women surprised me. She was incredibly forthcoming and charismatic, sharing with me that one day she wanted to work for me. She informed me that she had a bachelor's degree and had worked as a pharmacy tech for a large pharmacy chain. Her approach to excellence in her pharmacy tech position afforded her the opportunity to become a tech trainer. It was a shocking revelation and a reminder that you never truly know someone's story until you take the time to listen.

Despite her qualifications and previous successes, she had faced difficulties, and personal setbacks that knocked her off her feet. She had experienced hardship and loss, and insecurities and disappointment had taken their toll on her. In search of a fresh start, she moved to a different state and ended up at the organization where I worked. She was simply trying to pick up the pieces of her brokenness and find a new path forward.

It was no surprise to me that she, and many others, asked if they could work for me. I believe they were drawn to me because of the respect I showed them. In my own life, I have experienced the sting of being looked down upon and made to feel unimportant. As a poverty-stricken immigrant, many people disregarded me because of my circumstances. This has given me a deep love and respect for all humanity, regardless of title or position. I look for the underdog! Because they are usually the most appreciative, hardworking, and loyal.

It is my firm belief that we need to return to a culture of honoring and respecting each other, rather than seeking what we can gain from others. Everyone has a story, and we should never judge someone based on their current circumstances.

Take the time to talk to the person you think can do nothing for you because you will be surprised, they may become the next person who will give you a fresh start!

Discover the Game-Changing Strategy for Uniting Generations in the Workplace

As a leader in the workplace, I always strived to understand and connect with the multi-generational team members that I work with. Over the years, I have learned that the key to leading and inspiring a diverse group of individuals is rooted in respect, understanding, and building trust. This lesson was truly brought to life during my time working at the university and at various global organizations. I had the privilege of working with thousands of young people.

I quickly learned through observation that one of the greatest challenges for leaders of bridging the gap between different generations was (what appeared to me as) their unwillingness to connect with the younger talent genuinely and authentically. I realized that by investing just a little time and effort into building relationships with them through the vehicle of respect for their values, perspectives, ideas, innovation, and creativity, they became the most committed and loyal team members.

It was not about agreeing with everything they said, but it was about empathetically listening to understand their point of view, allowing them to express themselves without me feeling the need to constantly correct them. I also found that when I honored and valued their contributions to a project or in a meeting, they were in turn receptive to the wisdom and experiences that I imparted to them. It became clear to me that wisdom does not come with age, but rather with reflection on the experiences acquired with age.

Embracing this mindset, I learned that respect should be extended to everyone, from the janitor who fulfills their duties diligently, to the CEO leading the organization. You see, we have been conditioned to believe that respect is earned, and that is a dangerous hill to die on. If respect is easy to lose and difficult to gain, why are we setting people up for failure right away? Give respect first and instead of letting them earn it, give them the opportunity to lose it! This is the power of positive psychology.

You never know how each person's path may intersect with yours in the future. It's not always about what others can do for you, but what you can do for them.

I encourage you to ask yourself, what kind of person do you strive to be? Do you strive to be the kind of person who extends respect and understanding to others, even when they can offer you absolutely nothing in return? This is the mindset that has led me to connect and lead multi-generational teams successfully. I can attest that it pays dividends, not just in terms of professional success, but also on a personal level. I'd rather live a life of significance than a life of empty achievements.

Embrace this power for transformation on your teams and nurture a culture of inclusivity and mutual respect. When you strive to be the kind of person who respects and values others, it not only benefits the individuals around you but also fosters a positive and thriving organizational culture.

SELF-Checklist: Avoid These 15 Respect Blunders in the Workplace

- Assuming everyone shares the same cultural values and norms regarding respect.

- Interrupting colleagues when they are speaking.

- Using inappropriate or offensive language or jokes.

- Not actively listening to others during meetings or conversations.

- Ignoring or dismissing the ideas and opinions of others.

- Talking over or dominating conversations.

- Not acknowledging the contributions of others.

- Behaving in a condescending or patronizing manner.

- Not offering assistance or support to colleagues in need.

- Speaking negatively about colleagues behind their backs.

- Not considering the impact of your actions or words on others.

- Belittling or diminishing the accomplishments of others.

- Failing to take responsibility for mistakes and apologizing when necessary.

- Being late to meetings which communicates a lack of respect.

- Ignoring emails or not responding in a timely manner.

Generational Contributions Unveiled: 15 Workplace Skills from Traditionalists to Gen Z

As a transformational leader, it's important to recognize and appreciate the unique contributions each generation brings to the table. From the work ethic and loyalty of Traditionalists to the tech-savvy and collaborative nature of Millennials and Gen Z, each generation has something valuable to offer. This list will help you create a more inclusive and effective work environment by outlining the diverse ways each generation can enhance and improve your team, allowing you to better understand and leverage the skills and perspectives of all your employees.

Traditionalists (born 1928-1945)

- Strong work ethic and loyalty to the company

- Experience and wisdom that can serve as a mentorship to younger generations.

- Willingness to adhere to organizational structure and hierarchy.

- They are your rule followers.

Baby Boomers (born 1946-1964)

- Strong leadership skills and ability to inspire and motivate others.

- Experience in negotiation and conflict resolution.

- Driven by a desire to leave a legacy in their work.

- They are your workaholics.

Gen X (born 1965-1980)

- Adaptability and willingness to embrace change.

- Strong independent work ethic and creativity.

- Ability to balance work-life integration with a focus on family and personal well-being.

- They are your critical thinkers to get you out of a jam.

Millennials (born 1981-1996)

- Tech-savvy and skilled in using social media and digital platforms for marketing and networking.

- Fervent desire for inclusivity and diversity in the workplace.

- Emphasis on work-life balance and a desire for meaningful work.

- They are your dreamers/entrepreneurs.

Gen Z (born 1997-2012)

- Innovation and creativity in problem-solving.

- Natural ability to multitask and work efficiently with technology.

- Desire for flexible work arrangements and opportunities for advancement.

- They are your eager beavers ready for a new project.

The Power of Laughter: Leveraging Humor to Build Stronger Teams and Relationships

Working eight plus hours a day can feel like a life sentence without the possibility of parole. That is why it is so important to infuse a little humor into your work. Otherwise, you're just sitting there like a sad, wilted office plant, counting down the minutes until you can escape.

And let's be real, even Gen Z, with their short attention spans and TikTok obsessions, don't want to spend their precious hours at work feeling like they're serving a prison sentence. So, it is essential to infuse a little bit of fun into the workplace to keep everyone from losing their minds.

Now, I get it. Not everyone is a natural-born comedian, and that's okay. But, let's face it, we all have that one coworker who thinks they're the next stand-up superstar. Instead of rolling your eyes and groaning at their cheesy jokes, try to appreciate their effort. After all, everyone has their own style of communication, and humor just happens to be theirs.

And just because your boss does not appreciate your impression of Michael Scott from The Office doesn't mean you should stop trying to inject a little levity into the office.

Speaking of bosses, humor is a fantastic way to deliver feedback because sometimes it can be a tough pill to swallow, especially when it's criticism. Instead of making someone feel attacked or defensive, a well-placed joke can help lighten the mood and make the feedback more digestible. Of course, it's all about finding the right balance and not turning it into a total roast session. There is a time and a place for everything, so don't overdo it!

It is important to remember that not everyone appreciates sarcasm or finds certain topics funny. What might be an innocent joke to you could be offensive to someone else. So, it is crucial to be mindful of your audience and the context in which you're using humor. While laughter is indeed the best medicine, we should always strive to use it responsibly and respectfully.

Infusing a little humor into the workplace isn't just about making the workday more enjoyable. It is about creating an environment that is inclusive and respectful. Whether it's lightening the mood, improving communication, or delivering feedback, humor can be a powerful tool when used thoughtfully. So, let's all strive to bring a little laughter into our work lives, unless you're Gen Z, in which case, you do you!

Here are Ideas to Incorporate Fun:

- Start meetings with a lighthearted icebreaker or joke to set a positive tone.

- Encourage team members to share funny anecdotes or moments from their day during check-ins.

- Incorporate humorous memes or GIFs in emails or team communication channels.

- Schedule a "funny video of the week" break during virtual meetings to lighten the mood.

- Host a virtual "Funny Friday" event where team members can share jokes or funny stories.

- Create a "humor corner" in the office with a bulletin board for sharing funny quotes or cartoons.

- Use humorous illustrations or visuals in presentations or training materials.

- Bring in a professional comedian for a team-building event or virtual comedy show.

- Implement a "pun of the day" challenge where team members can submit their best puns.

- Host a "caption this" contest for team photos or funny images.

- Share light-hearted customer testimonials or positive feedback to celebrate wins.

- Create a "humor committee" to brainstorm and implement creative ways to infuse humor into the workday.

- Play humorous team-building games during in-person or virtual team meetings.

- Encourage team members to share their favorite funny podcasts, TV shows, or movies.

- Allow team members to decorate their workspaces with funny or quirky items to personalize their environment.

What will you incorporate immediately?

_____

_____

_____

_____

_____

_____

_____

Chapter 7.

Transforming the Workplace Through Recognition and Authenticity

Congratulations on reaching BONUS Chapter 7!

This chapter will help you:

1. Understand the power of recognition in transforming the workplace culture and fostering positivity, engagement, and productivity among employees from different generations.

2. Recognize the specific ways in which different generations value and perceive recognition, such as public accolades for Baby Boomers, private acknowledgments for Gen Xers, and real-time feedback for Millennials.

3. Tailor recognition efforts to meet the specific needs and motivations of each generation by identifying their desires from their work, organization, and leader.

4. Leverage tools and resources, such as employee surveys and flexible recognition programs, to navigate the complexities of recognition across generations and cater to the diverse needs of a multi-generational team.

> *According to a Gallup and Workhuman report in 2022, the translated cost savings impact of employee recognition is approximately $16.1M annually for every 10,000 employees.*

When leaders authentically recognize and appreciate their employees, it not only boosts morale but also fosters a positive work culture and saves the organization an exorbitant amount of money. There is a measurable business impact to gratitude. Transforming the workplace through recognition means creating a culture of appreciation and authenticity. When employees feel valued and appreciated, they are more motivated, engaged, and committed to their work and the organization. As a leader, it is your responsibility to foster an environment where recognition is given freely, authentically, and often.

*According to a 2024 Gallup report, **eight one percent** of leaders say recognition is not a major strategic priority for* *their organization. Two out of three leaders say there is no budget allocation for recognition.* And I have done extensive research on management training programs in organizations, and it is mind blowing that **seventy three percent** of leaders say there is no "best-practices" training around management for new or seasoned leaders.

Giving recognition is not just about praising employees for their hard work; it's also about knowing when to recognize them. *For example,* if an employee from the Baby Boomer generation goes above and beyond to complete a project, acknowledging their dedication and experience can go a long way. On the other hand, if a Millennial employee introduces a new and innovative idea, recognizing their creativity and forward-thinking mindset is crucial.

Give Recognition and Know When to Recognize Employees

No this is not an everyone gets a trophy for showing up to work section, this is simply an easy low cost, low effort, high return skill to master!

When is it appropriate to give recognition? Well, let's just say, anytime someone does something worth recognizing! Whether it's a big achievement like closing a major deal or a small act of kindness like bringing in donuts for the team, giving recognition is always appropriate. There are plenty of opportunities to show some love. Just keep it genuine and timely, and you'll be golden. After all, who doesn't love a little pat on the back for a job well done?

Now, why is it important to give recognition? It's simple, really. People work harder and feel more motivated when they know their efforts are being appreciated. Plus, it creates a positive and supportive work environment where everyone feels valued and recognized for their contributions. And let's be real, who doesn't want to work in a place like that?

So, what will recognition yield, you ask? Well, for starters, it will yield happier and more engaged employees. They will feel more connected to their work and the company, which can lead to increased productivity and better results. Not to mention, it can also improve employee retention because no one wants to leave a job where they feel appreciated. It's a win-win situation, my friends.

Seriously, there's never a wrong time to recognize someone for their hard work or dedication. It could be during a team meeting, in a team's virtual chat, in a company-wide email, or even just a quick thank you in passing. The important thing is to keep it real and keep it classy!

Each Generation Perceives Recognition Differently

As a leader, you can leverage various tools and resources to help navigate the complexities of recognition across generations. Understanding each generation's motivations, preferences, and expectations from their work efforts will be vital in your success as a leader when it comes to recognition. For instance, conducting employee surveys or feedback sessions can provide insight into the preferences and expectations of different generations. Additionally, implementing a flexible recognition program that includes a variety of rewards and acknowledgments can cater to the diverse needs of your multi-generational team.

For example, consider implementing a recognition program that includes a variety of methods, such as an "Employee of the Month" award for Baby Boomers, a "Spotlight on Success" for Generation X, and a social media shout-out for Millennials and Gen Z. This approach ensures that each generation feels valued and appreciated in a way that is meaningful to them.

I would also like to caution you to still individualize reward and recognition to personal preferences as well. If you and your team have completed their DiSC assessment, you may find out that some team members really do not like the spotlight. Proceed with caution as you certainly want to treat others how they want to be treated!

Avoid These 10 Common Mistakes When Affirming Employees from Different Generation

1. Avoid assuming all employees from the same generation will have the same values and motivations.

2. Avoid relying on stereotypes or generalizations about different generations in the workplace.

3. Avoid favoritism towards employees from your own generation.

4. Do not underestimate the value of diversity in the workplace, including generational diversity.

5. Avoid assuming that younger employees are more tech-savvy or innovative than older employees.

6. Do not overlook the potential for mentorship and learning from employees of different generations.

7. Do not overlook the unique perspectives and experiences that employees from different generations can bring to the table.

8. Avoid assuming that younger employees are less committed or loyal to the company.

9. Avoid assuming that older employees are less adaptable/teachable and are resistant to change or innovative ideas.

10. Don't dismiss the potential for creativity and innovation from employees of different generations.

Creating a Connected Workplace: The Ultimate Shopping List for Recognizing Different Generations

1. Personalized notes of appreciation - For *Traditionalists*, a handwritten note expressing gratitude for their hard work and dedication will go a long way in making them feel valued.

2. Recognition luncheons - *Baby Boomers* appreciate formal recognition events such as luncheons where their achievements are celebrated in front of their colleagues.

3. Flexible work arrangements - *Gen X and Millennial* employees value work-life balance, so offering flexible work arrangements as a form of recognition can boost morale and show appreciation for their productivity.

4. Social media shoutouts – *Millennials and Gen Z* enjoy public recognition, so giving them a shoutout on the company's social media platforms can make them feel appreciated and recognized.

5. Mentorship opportunities - *Millennials and Gen Z* employees value growth and development, so offering mentorship opportunities as a form of recognition can show them that their contributions are valued and that the company invests in their future.

6. Time off awards - Offering *Traditionalists* additional vacation time as a form of recognition can show them that their hard work is valued and that the company respects their need for rest and relaxation.

7. Employee of the Month programs - *Baby Boomers* appreciate structured recognition programs, and an employee of the month program can provide them with a tangible form of recognition for their efforts.

8. Team building activities – *Millennials and Gen Z* enjoy collaborative and team-oriented recognition, so organizing team building activities can provide them with a sense of camaraderie and appreciation for their contributions.

9. Personalized awards - Creating personalized awards for *Gen Z* employees can show them that their unique skills and talents are recognized and valued within the organization.

10. Public recognition at company meetings - *Traditionalists* appreciate public and formal recognition, so acknowledging their achievements in front of their colleagues at company meetings can make them feel appreciated and respected.

11. Bonuses and financial rewards – I don't know of anyone who does not like financial rewards, so offering

bonuses or financial incentives for their performance can show them that their hard work is valued.

12. Wellness initiatives - *Gen X* employees appreciate recognition that considers their overall well-being, so implementing wellness initiatives such as gym memberships or wellness days can demonstrate appreciation for their health and happiness.

Recognition and authenticity are powerful tools that leaders can use to transform their workplaces. By understanding the nuances of recognition across different generations and tailoring your approach accordingly, you can create a positive and inclusive work culture that resonates with all employees.

Recognition is not just a formality, but a genuine expression of appreciation and gratitude that can lead to greater employee engagement and ultimately, a high-performing, cohesive, and successful multi-generational team.

As you continue your journey to become a respected multigenerational executive leader, remember that genuine recognition and affirmation of your employees can lead to a more inspired and motivated workforce.

A little gratitude can change anyone's attitude.
Positive words of affirmation and positive thinking
puts you in forward momentum.

Conclusion

Congratulations on completing "Bridge the Gap Lead the Pack: 5 Bullet-Proof Ways to Connect and Lead Multi-Generations in the Workplace"! I hope you found the book to be a valuable resource in navigating and leading multi-generational teams in the workplace.

As a leader, you understand the challenges that come with effectively communicating and leading a workforce made up of different generations. But you have also gained valuable insight into how to bridge the gap and lead the pack in this dynamic and ever-changing workplace environment.

Throughout this book, you've learned practical advice, tips, and tricks to connect and lead multi-generational teams with confidence. I hope that you have found the information to be not only informative but also actionable. You've explored the importance of emotional intelligence, building trust, and understanding the unique perspectives and values of each generation.

You've also discovered strategies for effective communication that resonate with every member of your team. You've delved into concepts like the effectiveness of assessments, and the power of coaching vs managing. And I believe you are now equipped with the knowledge and tools to drive profitability and organizational success in rapidly changing times.

It is now time to put your newfound knowledge into action. I encourage you to take the next step and implement at least one new strategy for improved communication within your team. Whether it is implementing a mentorship program, adopting a coaching style of leadership, organizing intergenerational teamwork activities, or simply adjusting your communication style to better fit the preferences of each generation. Acting **NOW** is key to seeing real change in your workplace dynamics.

In addition to implementing new strategies, I invite you to visit my website for helpful resources and to schedule a free consultation to move you forward in YOUR leadership journey. I am here to support you and I am committed to helping you bridge the gap and lead the pack in your organization.

Remember, lead with confidence. By embracing the principles and strategies outlined in this book, you will not only drive profitability and organizational success, but also create a positive and inclusive work environment for everyone.

I wish you all the best in your leadership endeavors. Here's to connecting and leading multi-generations in the workplace!

Cheers!

Introducing Leoni Michael

Unleash the Power of Multi-Generational Leadership with Leoni Michael - A Leader for Leaders

In *"Bridge the Gap Lead the Pack: 5 Bullet-Proof Ways to Connect and Lead Multi-Generations in the Workplace,"* Leoni Michael delivers a groundbreaking guide for leaders struggling to connect and lead across multiple generations.

Drawing on her extensive experience in various industries and her expertise in business, psychology, and talent management, she provides a roadmap for effective leadership in this rapidly changing landscape of the modern workplace.

Leoni's motivation for writing this book stems from her passion for helping leaders successfully navigate and lead multi-generational teams, develop, and empower the next generation of leaders to thrive in the face of rapid change. She understands the challenges that leaders face in bridging the gap between different generations and aims to provide practical strategies for achieving success in this endeavor.

As a well-rounded executive leader with a diverse background in B2B, the medical field, beauty industry, retail, real estate, higher education, and entrepreneurship, Leoni brings a wealth of firsthand experience to the table. Her educational background in nursing, business management, human resource management, and industrial/organizational psychology, along with her certifications as a John Maxwell trainer, speaker, and executive coach, equips her with the knowledge and skills needed to help leaders effectively lead and communicate with any generation in the workplace.

With her expertise as a certified DiSC consultant and her prior role as a Director of Career Development at an accredited university, Leoni is uniquely positioned to guide leaders in connecting and leading multi-generational teams. Her experience as a leader in learning and development in global organizations further solidifies her credibility in this domain.

Join Leoni on social media to stay updated on the latest insights and strategies for multi-generational leadership.

For leaders seeking to bridge the gap in a multi-generational workplace, "Bridge the Gap Lead the Pack" is a must-read!

References

Introduction

UNLEASHING THE HUMAN ELEMENT AT WORK: Transforming Workplaces Through Recognition. Retrieved from unleashing-the-human-element-at-work-transforming-workplaces-through-recognition-2.pdf

Chapter 2

Goleman, D. (2020). *Emotional intelligence*. Bloomsbury.

Chapter 3

Maxwell, J. C. (2022). *The 15 invaluable laws of growth: Live them and reach your potential*. Center Street.

Chapter 7

UNLEASHING THE HUMAN ELEMENT AT WORK: Transforming Workplaces Through Recognition. Retrieved from unleashing-the-human-element-at-work-transforming-workplaces-through-recognition-2.pdf

Offers

#1 ❄ *Unleash the Power of Leadership with 100+ Coaching Questions!* ❄

Are you struggling to effectively lead your multi-generational teams in the workplace? Want to experience the true value of leadership as a leader that empowers and inspires growth and development that leads to each employee's success? Don't be at a loss for words or effective coaching questions any longer!

Download our FREE eBook: "100+ Powerful Coaching Questions" and learn how to build strong, effective generational teams, empower your employees, accelerate performance, and thrive in the workplace.

If you want even more 1:1 Coaching training, visit www.LeoniMichaelConsulting.com for exclusive deals.

Take the first step towards becoming a leader that makes a

real difference. ***Download the free eBook now*** and revolutionize the way you lead your teams!

#2 ❋ *Unleash the Power of Leadership with your DiSC Assessment!* ❋

Are you struggling to effectively lead your multi-generational team through effective communication and motivation? Do you find it challenging to connect with people of all different personality styles? It's time to take charge of your leadership skills with a DISC assessment and full 30-page report.

By understanding your own strengths and weaknesses, you can become a more effective leader. With the DISC assessment, you will learn about your communication style, motivation factors, and blind spots. This valuable insight will help you connect with your team on a deeper level and effectively lead them towards success.

The best part? You can do it all from the comfort of your home, without wasting time trying to figure out what the next generations are thinking. The assessment is quick and easy, and the full report will provide you with actionable insights that you can start implementing immediately.

But that's not all - if you're interested in taking your leadership skills to the next level, you can book a 45-minute debriefing coaching session with me, Leoni. Together, we can set you up for success and ensure that you're on the right track to becoming the best leader you can be.

Don't let ineffective communication and motivation hold you back. Take the first step towards becoming a better leader today. ***Take the assessment and receive the full report***, and let's work together to grow in your strengths and become a more effective communicator.